Knot Design

Kristin Möller

Knot Design

Original Key Chains, Cell Phone Cases, and Bracelets

Schiffer Publishing Ltd
4880 Lower Valley Road, Atglen, Pennsylvania 19310

Contents

Modern Knot Ideas

Everyone knows knotting – either as a useful aid in everyday life or as decorative knotting to embellish crafts. In the 1970s and 1980s, macramé knots were very popular. However, I did not catch the knotting fever until the beginning of the 1990s. On the one hand, I was inspired by the artistic hanging baskets that my grandfather made; on the other hand, friendship bracelets were in style. After I learned how to knot, I made different models, for example, bracelets, vests, and shoulder bags. Disappointed, I realized that, in the meantime, no one was interested in the "antiquated" macramé models any longer. My mother then advised me to create modern accessories. After I developed different cell phone and key cases in contemporary color combinations, more and more knot ideas came to me, and thus this book was made.

Kristin Möller
www.knuepfereien.de

With this book, I present to you a new, modern variety of knotting and wish you much fun recreating the work!

Yours,

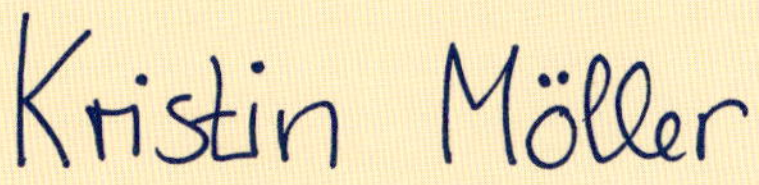

Materials & Aids

Materials

Most models are knotted with cotton thread (approximate length 410 feet (125 m) per $1^3/_4$ oz. (50 g), which is available in arts and crafts stores. Additional materials, such as split rings, snap hooks, side release buckles, buttons, and carrying straps, can be found in specialized hobby stores or home improvement stores.

Aids

The following aids are consistently required and, therefore, are not additionally listed in the individual instructions:

- Knotting pillow, approximately $15^3/_4$ x $15^3/_4$ inches (40 cm x 40 cm), to support the knot work,
- Measuring tape for cutting the threads,
- Safety pin to secure the model on the knotting pillow,
- Craft scissors (sharp) for cutting the threads and for cutting off stitched-up threads,
- Embroidery needle with a blunt tip so that the weave that is already knotted is not damaged,
- Flat nose pliers to stitch up the threads. With pliers it is easier to pull the embroidery needle through the tightly knotted weave.

Knotting Diagrams

- For each model there is a colored knotting diagram, or rather a type of numbered pattern, on which the knots are marked. The knotting diagrams display either the entire model (friendship bracelets) or – like with the cases – specific parts of the model.
- For the cases, first knot the base of the case; for this, turn the knotting diagram in the corresponding direction (symbol: black arrow). The numbers on the border indicate the rounds, or rather rows; short black dashes mark the respective beginning of the round, or rather row; long lines indicate the position of the slots for the split ring. Also, for the finishing knot there is a corresponding symbol (circle). So that the knotting diagram remains clear, the vertical half hitch knots are represented by little empty boxes; the little boxes for the horizontal half hitch knots are marked with an "x."

Levels of Difficulty

The models are grouped into the following levels of difficulty:

◆ easily made
◆◆ somewhat more difficult
◆◆◆ challenging

The Most Important Knots

For each knot, use two threads, the knotting cord, and the core cord: The knotting cord determines the color of the knot. The even, tight pulling of the knotting cord influences the structure of the finished model.

Vertical Half Hitch Knot, Knotted Right

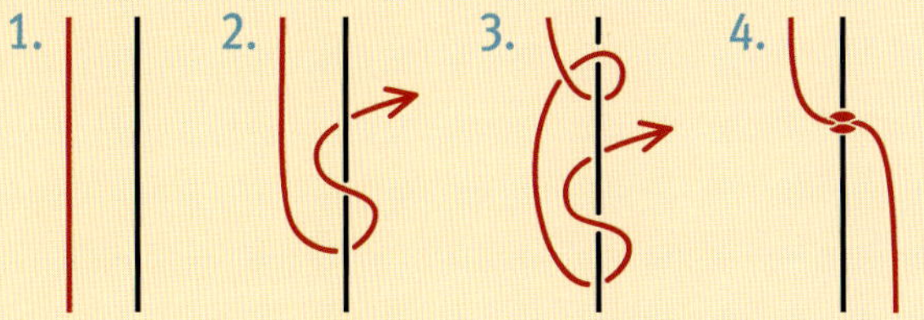

Tightly pull down the core cord (black). Wrap the knotting cord (red) around the core cord once, bring to the right, and tighten upwards. Make a loop to the right around the core cord once more with the knotting cord, and pull up evenly. The knotting cord (red) is now to the right of the core cord.

Vertical Half Hitch Knot, Knotted Left

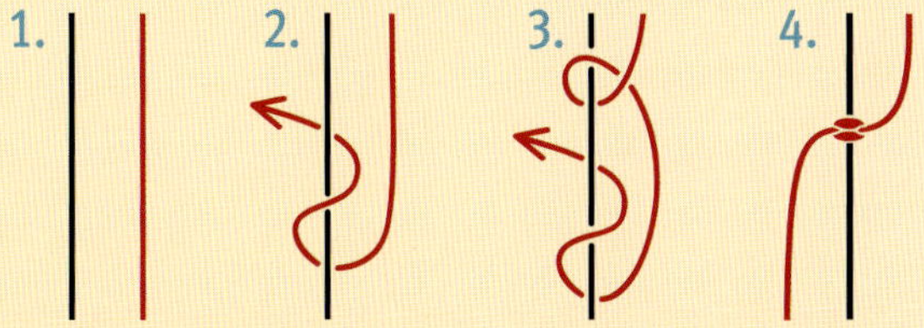

Tightly pull down the core cord (black). Wrap the knotting cord (red) around the core cord once, bring to the left, and tighten upwards. Make a loop to the left around the core cord once more with the knotting cord, and pull up evenly. The knotting cord (red) is now to the left of the core cord.

Horizontal Half Hitch Knot, Knotted Right

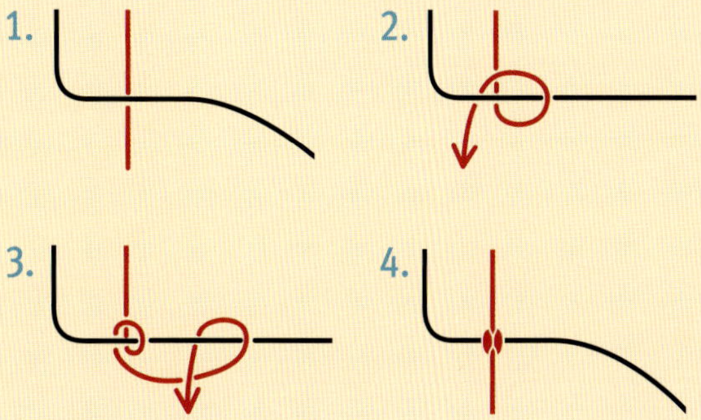

Place the core cord (black) to the right. Wrap the knotting cord (red) around the core cord once and pull downwards. Make a loop around the core cord once again with the knotting cord and pull downwards evenly.

Horizontal Half Hitch Knot, Knotted Left

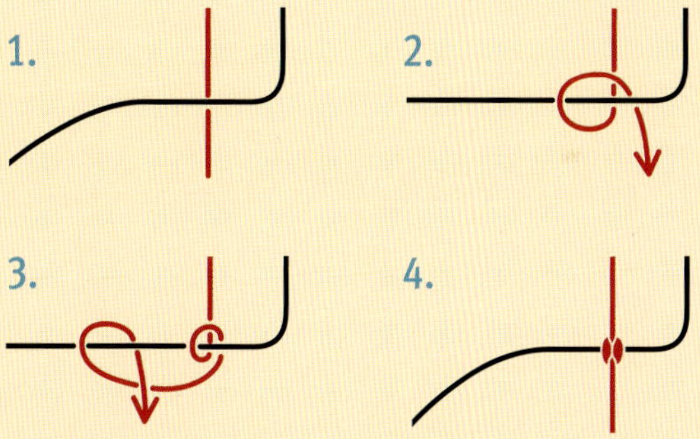

Place the core cord (black) to the left. Wrap the knotting cord (red) around the core cord once and pull downwards. Make a loop around the core cord once again with the knotting cord and pull downwards evenly.

Spiral Knot, Knotted Right

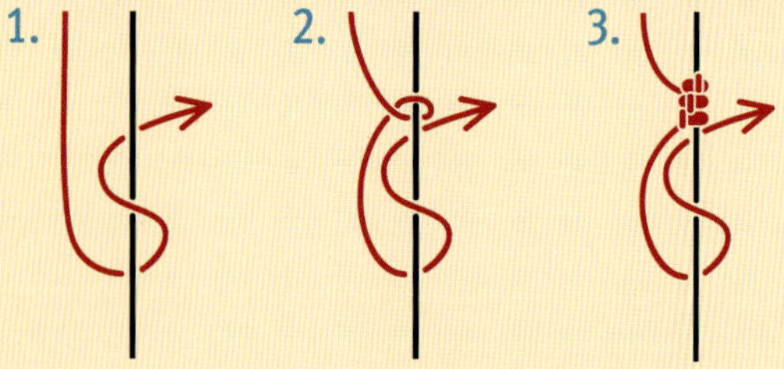

Knot several consecutive vertical half hitch knots, knotted right, over the same core cord. After approximately 5 repetitions, the resulting structure begins to turn spirally around the core cord. Hence the name for this knot.

Spiral Knot, Knotted Left

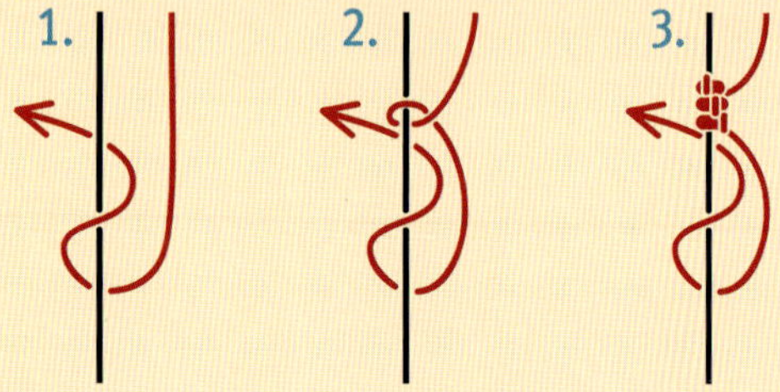

Make several consecutive vertical half hitch knots, knotted left, over the same core cord. After approximately 5 repetitions a spiral structure is also formed here.

Tip

If you knot according to a specified pattern (knotting diagram) it will become apparent during production if you will have to use a vertical or horizontal half hitch knot towards the left or right.

Square Knot

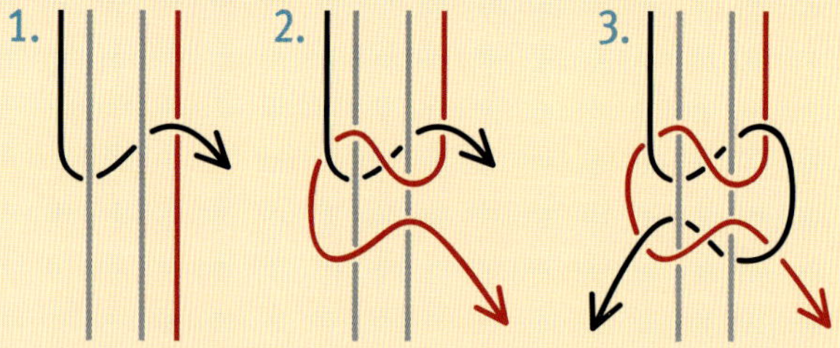

1. The square knot consists of two core cords (inside) and two knotting cords (outside). Tightly pull down both core cords in the center. Bring the left knotting cord towards the right under both core cords and over the right knotting cord.

2. Bring the right knotting cord towards the left over both core cords and under the left knotting cord. Tighten both outer threads evenly. These threads have switched their position. Bring the knotting cord (red) now lying to the left over the center core cords.

3. Bring this knotting cord towards the right under the knotting cord (black) now lying to the right. Bring the right knotting cord (black) under both core cords and through the resulting loop of the left knotting cord through the bottom to the left.

4. Now tighten both outer threads evenly. The knotting cords are once again in their starting position.

Finishing Knot

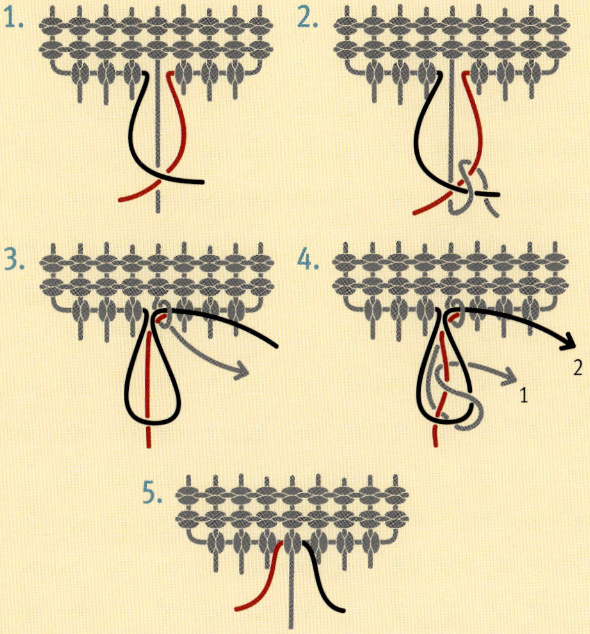

All sections of a model end with a final row. Knot the last row from each side towards the center with horizontal half hitch knots.

1. Put both core cords crosswise in the center and pull tightly.

2. Bring the center thread around both crossed core cords and pull downwards.

3. Bring the center core cord around the crossed threads once more and pull downwards.

4. Tighten the threads in the specified sequence (1, 2).

5. The final row is now closed and the threads can be stitched up.

Attaching the Threads

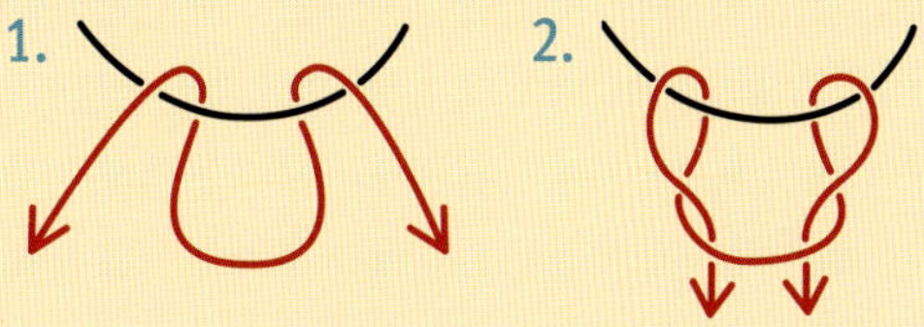

For some models, for example, the lanyards, the threads are attached to a key ring or snap hook.

1. Fold the thread in half and bring the resulting loop over the key ring/snap hook.

2. Pull the resulting loop downwards behind the key ring/snap hook. Bring the thread ends that are above the key ring/snap hook downwards through the formed loop. Pull both thread ends downwards.

Winding the Threads

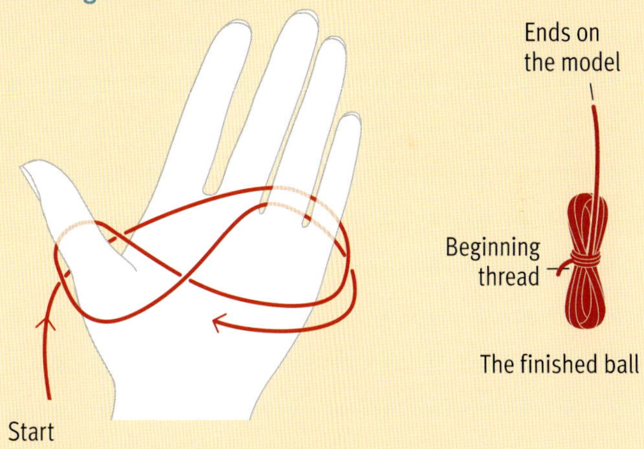

Wind the very long knotting cords like in the illustration, leaving approximately 5⅞ inches (15 cm) out at the beginning. Tie together the formed ball with this piece of thread. As soon as the thread becomes too short during knotting, simply pull on the small ball and thus extend the thread.

Basic Course In Cases

Fundamental Tips

- Always knot all cases in the same sequence: Begin with the base and knot it in rows from left to right. Then make the body of the case, using all core cords of the base for the side walls of the case, much like basket weaving. Lastly, make the case flap with the clasp.
- Make the cases clockwise in rounds with two knotting cords offset laterally, or in forward and backward rows with horizontal and vertical half hitch knots. The pattern emerges from the different colors of the threads and types of knots.
- Always use two knotting cords; one thread is for the even rounds, and the other thread is for the odd rounds. With only one knotting cord, the cases would distort into a spiral. Each new round always begins between two vertical half hitch knots, so that later, the transition from round to round is not visible on the finished case.
- Because the knotting cords are sometimes very long, it makes sense to separate the threads into several small strands and add a new thread in between. Always stitch up the beginning threads after 2 or 3 rounds.
- If a thread has accidentally ended up too short, simply knot on a new piece in the next row/round with the appropriate knot of the pattern. Stitch up the thread right after 2 or 3 rounds/rows here, too.
- When stitching up the threads make sure not to pull the thread on the back side through the loop of the knot, from where the beginning or end of the thread originates; otherwise, the knotted weave can come undone.
- The size of the case depends on the number of core cords. The more core cords used, the wider the case will be. The height of the case is also variable and can be changed by the number of rounds/rows.

Special note: Conversions were made from metric system to inches/feet/ounces, etc., and are not exact.

Layout for This Example

- Core cords for the base and body of the case
- 2 knotting cords for the body of the case
- 1 knotting cord for the flap
- The exact specifications for the number and length of the thread are stated in the instructions of the respective models. The base of the case in this example consists of 4 lengthwise threads and 9 horizontal threads

The Base of the Case

1. Cut the core cords to the specified length, knot together in the center, and secure on the knotting pillow with a safety pin. Fold the remaining core cords in half and consecutively knot on from left to right so that, on both sides, the thread is approximately the same length.

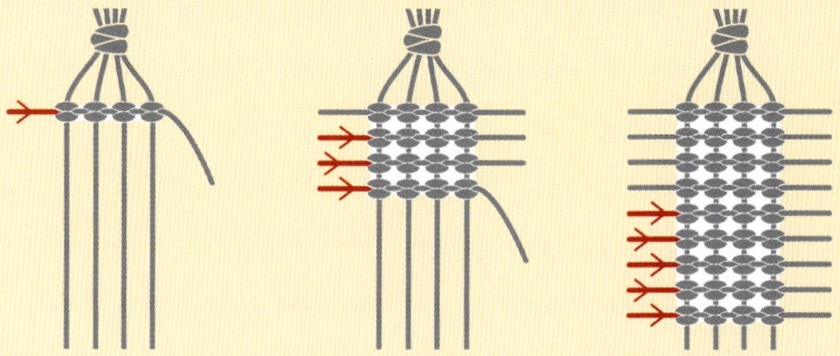

2. Release the completely knotted base from the safety pin and spread out all core cords on the knotting pillow unsecured for the time being.

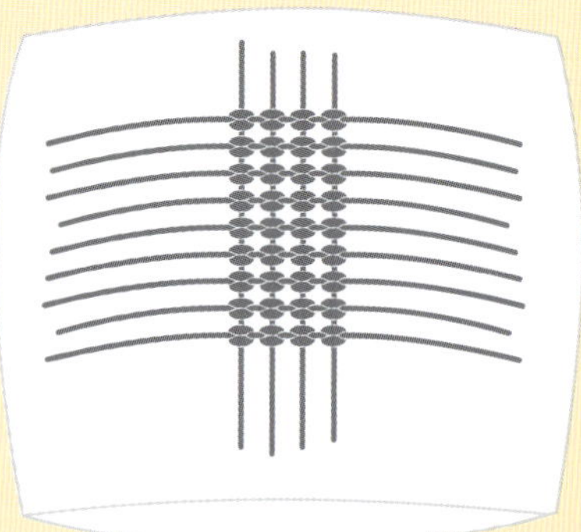

Knotting pillow

The Body of the Case

1. Begin the first round with one of the two knotting cords (symbol in the knotting diagram: short, black, vertical dash). For the first round, the work piece remains unsecured on the knotting pillow for the time being.

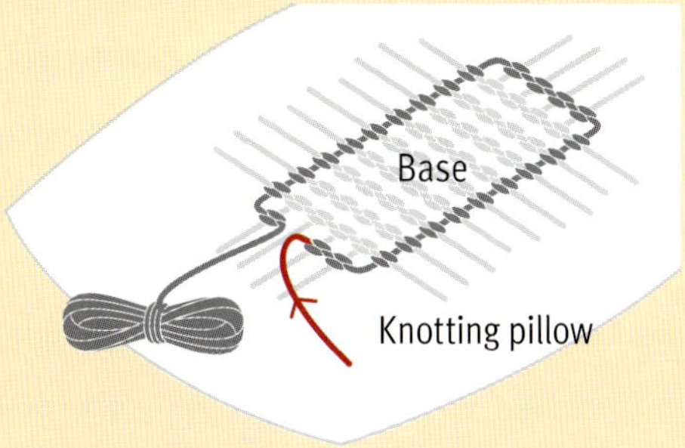

2. After the 1st round, pull through two auxiliary threads at the marked location (see knotting diagram) with the embroidery needle. Knot the auxiliary threads and secure the beginning of the case on the knotting pillow with a safety pin. Thus, it is easier to continue knotting because the threads lie neatly next to each other on the knotting pillow. The body of the case becomes so high with an increasing number of rounds that it would constantly fall over while knotting without auxiliary threads.

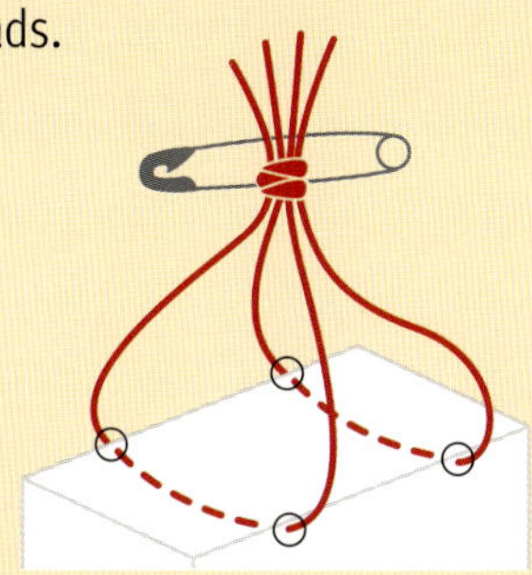

3. Now alternating with both knotting cords, work the rounds for the body of the case offset laterally. One thread is used for the even rounds and the other thread for the odd rounds.

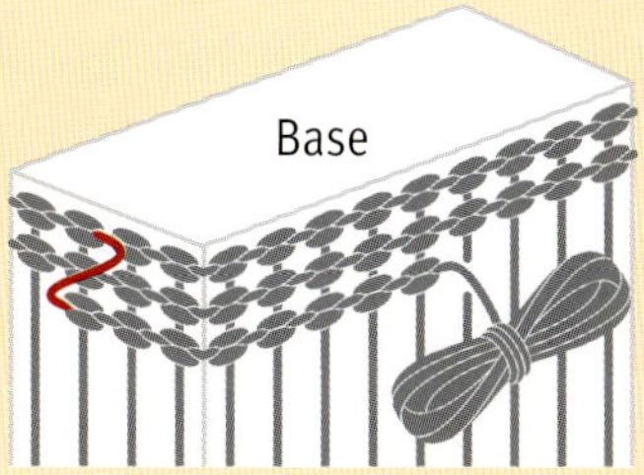

4. After the 5th or 6th round, release the case from the safety pin, turn inside out, and stitch up the beginning threads on the inside.

5. Secure the case on the knotting pillow with the safety pin again. Continue knotting according to the knotting diagram up to the marked beginning of the flap for the key ring. Clip off the knotting cords and stitch up. If the finished case will not have a key ring, simply continue knotting following the pattern.

Making the Key Ring Flap

1. For many models a flap (between two slots) is knotted for a key ring. The position of the slots are marked on the knotting diagrams. On one side of a slot, add a new knotting cord. Work the following rows according to the pattern in forward and backward rows.

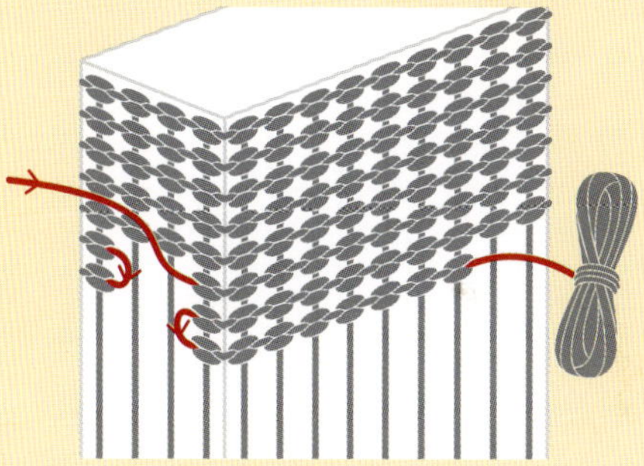

2. Knot the flap over the threads between the slots with the longer knotting cord in forward and backward rows. Then clip off the threads and stitch up all beginning and ending threads on the inside. Pull the key ring on the knotted flap.

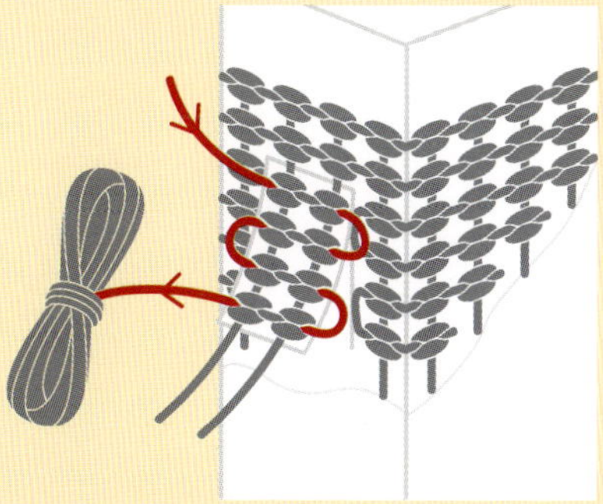

3. Additional rounds follow that are again worked clockwise alternating with both knotting cords. Then stitch up the knotting cords.

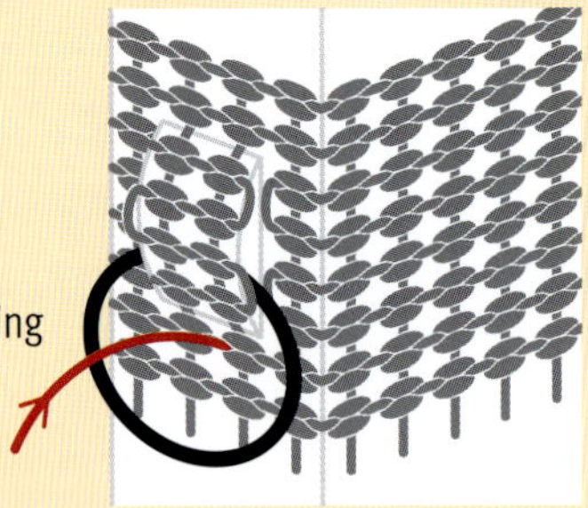

The Clasp Flap

1. On the back side of the case, separate the center threads for the clasp flap. In doing so, on both sides of the flap add a thread of the side sections. Attach the knotting cord on the left and knot the clasp flap over these threads in forward and backward rows (also see knotting diagram).

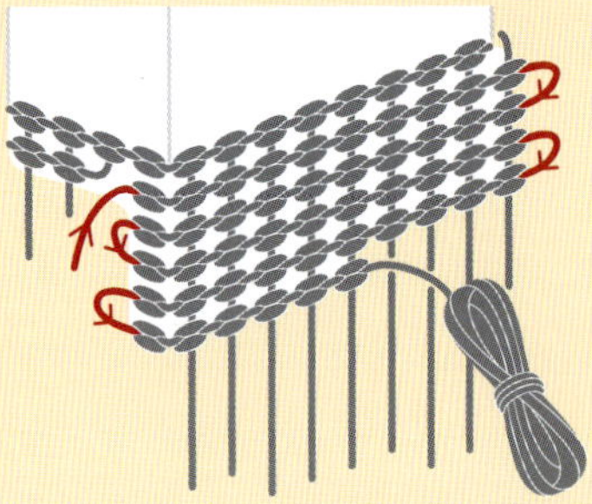

2. Finish the flap with a final row. In doing so, knot horizontal half hitch knots towards the center over both outermost core cords. End the last row with a finishing knot.

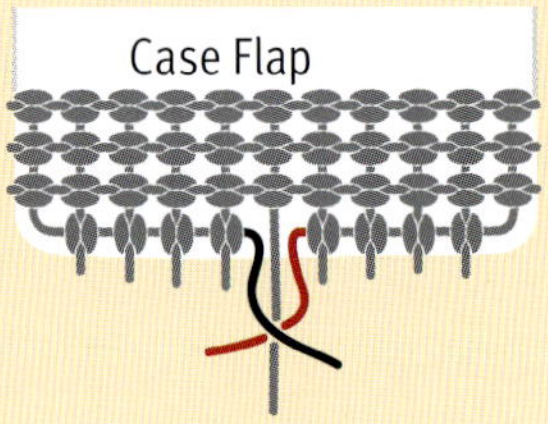

Different Clasps

For the clasp, either knot a loop out of three threads, work an elastic band into the flap while knotting, attach a snap fastener, or sew on a side release buckle.

- For the **loop**, make spiral knots on the end of the flap with one thread over the two right adjacent threads. Stitch up the thread ends on the inside at an even distance. Thus, a knotted loop develops to close the case.

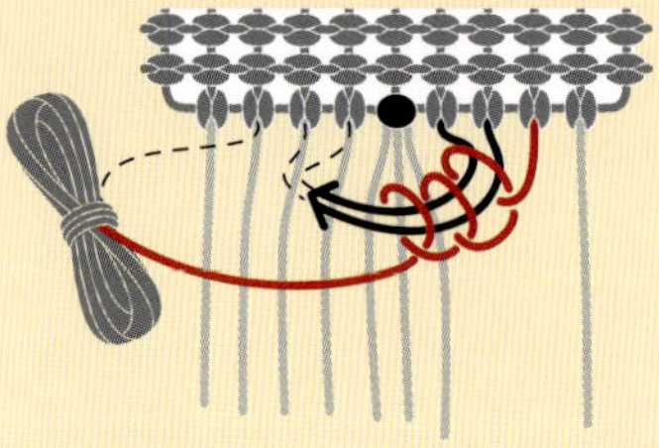

- Knot in the **elastic band** when finishing the case flap. On the marked locations on the knotting diagram add the elastic band to the core cord and knot over both with the appropriate knotting cord.

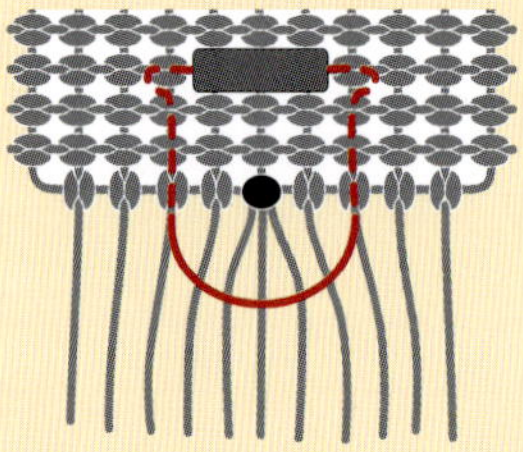

- Attach a **snap fastener** with special pliers after the completion of the case flap.

• To be able to attach a **side release buckle,** first knot on a narrow flap in forward and backward rows on the case flap. Pull the resulting flap from the top towards the bottom through the side release buckle.

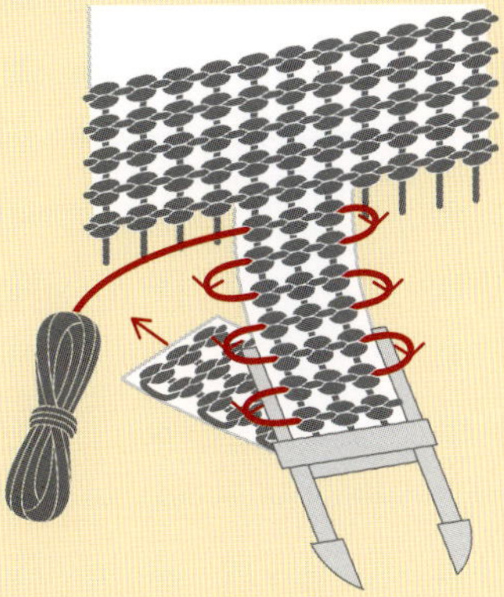

On the inside of the case flap stitch up the flap's core cords well.

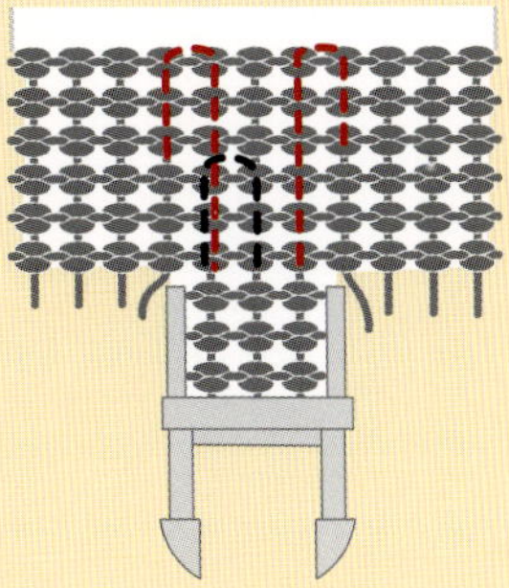

With the core cords knot a final row on each right and left side of the side release buckle that will be completed with a finishing knot.

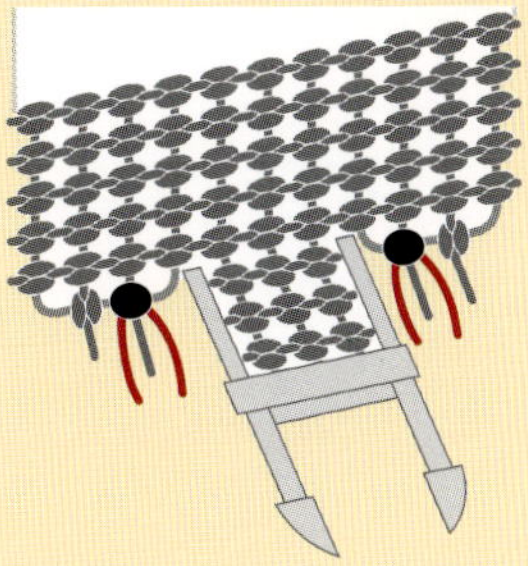

Completing the Case

1. Turn the case in such a way that the front side is at the top. Now with the core cords of the side sections and the front side, also knot a final row. For this, make horizontal half hitch knots towards the center over the outermost core cords.

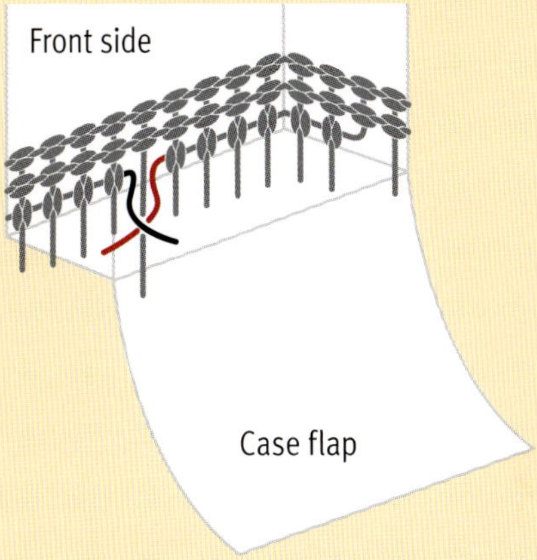

2. Lastly, clip off all threads except for approximately 4 inches (10 cm) and stitch up on the inside. For this, pull the thread through with the embroidery needle under the back side of 3 knots.

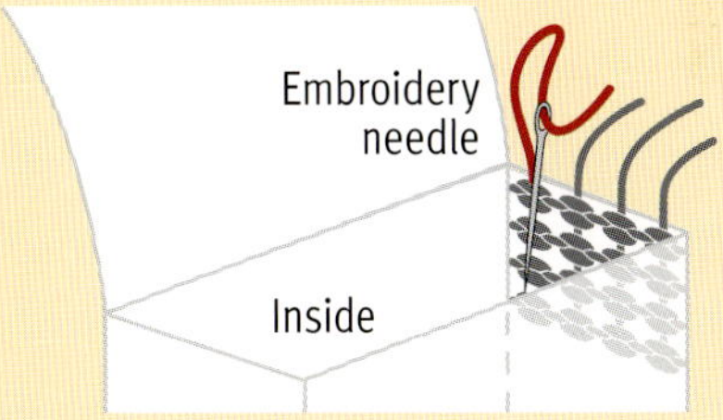

Friendship Bracelets

Materials

Semicircle Pattern

- $1\frac{3}{4}$ oz. (50 g) cotton each in black
- Different thread remnants in white, beige, gray tones

Checked Pattern

- $1\frac{3}{4}$ oz. (50 g) cotton each in black, light green

Zigzag Pattern

- $1\frac{3}{4}$ oz. (50 g) cotton each in grass-green, light green

Thread Layout

Semicircle Pattern

- 8 core cords (thread remnants), about 4 feet (1.30 m)
- Knotting cord in black, about 18 feet (5.60 m)

Checked Pattern

- 8 core cords in light green, about $3\frac{1}{2}$ feet (1.10 m) each
- Knotting cord in black, about $16\frac{1}{2}$ feet (5 m)

Zigzag Pattern

- 9 core cords in grass-green, about 4 feet (1.30 m) each
- Knotting cord in light green, about $20\frac{1}{2}$ feet (6 m)

Size

- $6\frac{1}{8}$ inches (15.5 cm)

Level of Difficulty

◆

1. Knot together 8 threads for the semicircle and checked patterns and 9 threads for the zigzag pattern after approximately 2 inches (5 cm) and secure on the knotting pillow with a safety pin.

2. Begin on the left with the knotting cord and work 37 forward and 37 backward rows (only 36 rows for the checked pattern) with horizontal and vertical half hitch knots as per the knotting diagrams (basic instructions, pages 6 - 9).

3. Finally, make a braid on both sides of the bracelets: For this, separate three strands, braid $3\frac{1}{8}$ inches (8 cm), and knot together.

Semicircle Pattern

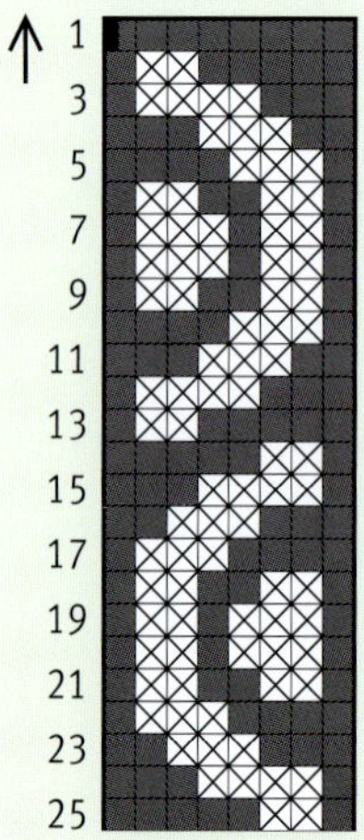

Repeat rows 2 - 25 (2x)

Checked Pattern

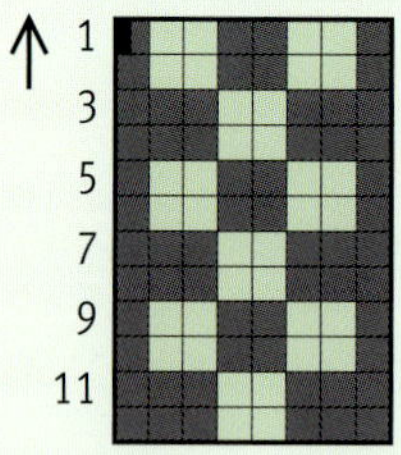

Repeat rows 1 - 12 (5x)

Zigzag Pattern

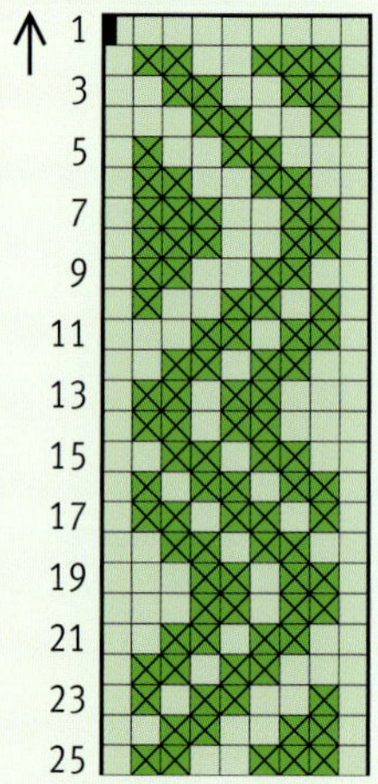

Repeat rows 2 - 25 (2x)

Key

- ↑ Direction
- ◧ Beginning of row
- ☒ Horizontal half hitch knot
- ☐ Vertical half hitch knot

Diagonal Strips

Materials

- $1^{3}/_{4}$ oz. (50 g) cotton each in gray (pink), dark gray (green mottled pattern)
- Snap fastener "color" in black or dark green, $^{1}/_{8}$ inch (3 mm) dia.
- Key ring, approximately $^{1}/_{2}$ inch (18 mm) dia.

Thread Layout

For the Base and Case

- 31 core cords in gray (pink), about 4 feet (1.30 m) each
- 2 knotting cords in dark gray (green mottled pattern), about 28 feet (8.50 m) each

For the Flap

- Knotting cord in dark gray (green mottled pattern), about 17 feet (5.30 m)

Size

- $2^{1}/_{8}$ x $2^{5}/_{8}$ x $^{1}/_{4}$ inches (5.5 cm x 6.7 cm x 0.6 cm) (W x H x D)

Level of Difficulty

◆◆

1. According to the basic instructions (pages 6 - 13) make the base of the case from 31 core cords (3 vertical threads, 28 horizontal threads). Now work the case per round alternating with one of the two dark gray (green mottled pattern) knotting cords offset laterally. After the 5th or 6th round, stitch up the beginning threads on the inside. As per the knotting pattern, continue working through round 27 and stitch up the knotting cords.

2. Work in both slots for the split ring on the back side of the case (see basic instructions, page 11), here separating the center 10 threads for the flap between the slots. On one side of a slot, newly add the knotting cord. Work the following rows as per the knotting diagram. Knot the flap for the split ring with the longer knotting cord over the 10 threads between the slots. Pull the split ring on the knotted flap. Work two more rounds clockwise alternating with both knotting cords. After the 31st round, stitch up all the beginning and ending threads on the inside. For the clasp flap on the back side of the case, separate the 30 center threads (basic instructions, page 12) and knot 11 forward and 10 backward rows. Then knot the final rows for all sections according to the basic instructions. Attach the snap fastener.

The knotting diagram shows the base, the back side with the case flap, and the side sections. The front and back sides are identical.

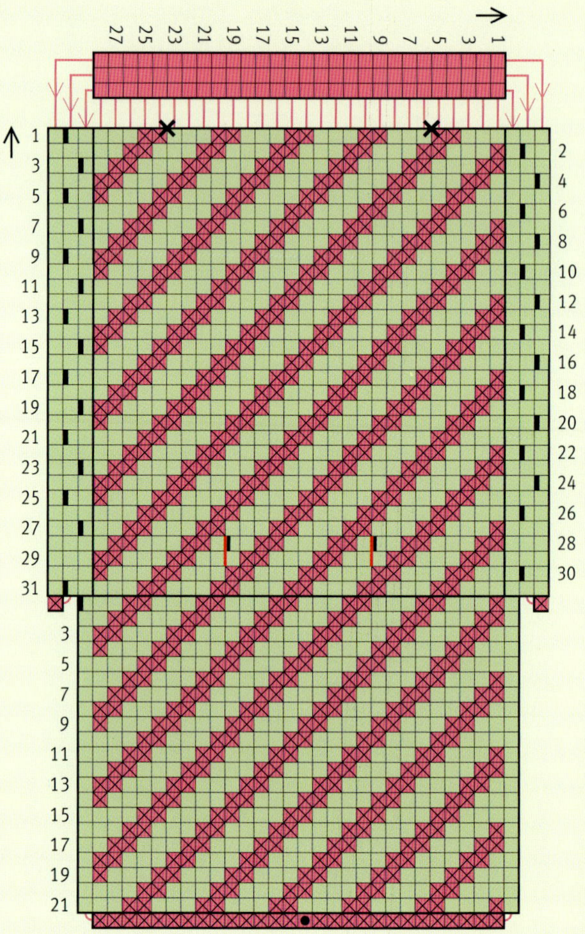

Key

- ↑ Direction
- ◧ Beginning of round, or rather row
- × Auxiliary thread
- ☒ Horizontal half hitch knot
- ☐ Vertical half hitch knot
- ◙ Finishing knot
- | Include slot

JOE COOMER
Die

Decorative Hangers

Materials

For All Models

- Snap hook, approximately 1 1/2 inches (4 cm) long
- Leather strap in brown or black
- Wooden beads (for exact specifications, see knotting diagram)

Green-Blackberry

- 1 3/4 oz. (50 g) cotton in blackberry, green

Light Brown

- 1 3/4 oz. (50 g) cotton in light brown

Turquoise-Blackberry

- 1 3/4 oz. (50 g) cotton in blackberry, turquoise

Thread Layout & Knotting Diagrams

Page 20

Size

Green-Blackberry:

- 2 inches (5 cm)

Light Brown:

- 3 1/2 inches (9 cm)

Turquoise-Blackberry:

- 8 1/4 inches (21 cm)

Level of Difficulty

◆◆

1. First complete the loops that will be connected to the snap hook: For the green-blackberry hanger, gather together the leather strap and the green thread and work 30 spiral knots with a thread in blackberry over the center (instructions page 8). For the light brown hanger, use a light brown knotting cord, for the turquoise-blackberry hanger use a turquoise-colored knotting cord. Place the knotted-over leather strap with the threads through the snap hook.

2. Make the spiral knot strands according to the specifications on the knotting diagram. Arrange the beads at the marked locations. Finally, tightly knot the strap above and below the beads.

Tip

On the knotting diagram, the numbers are next to the strands for the number of spiral knots, which are made over the remaining threads, thereby one thread is always the knotting cord, the remaining threads become the core cords. So that the threads are evenly used, the same color threads should be switched after each step.

Green-blackberry

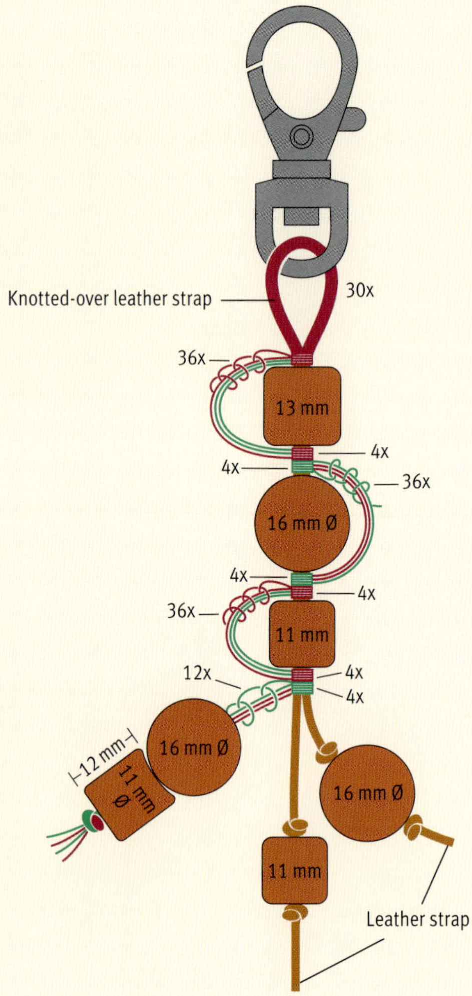

Thread Layout and Knotting Diagrams for "Decorative Hangers" (Page 18)

Thread Layout

Green-Blackberry

- Thread in blackberry, about 7 feet (2.20 m)
- Thread in green, about 7 feet (2.20 m)
- Brown leather strap, 15 3/4 inches (40 cm)

Light Brown

- 2 threads in light brown, about 6 1/2 feet (2 m) each
- Black leather strap, 23 5/8 inches (60 cm)

Turquoise-Blackberry

- 2 threads in blackberry, about 8 feet (2.50 m) each
- 2 threads in turquoise, about 8 feet (2.50 m) each
- Brown leather strap, 23 5/8 inches (60 cm)

Light Brown

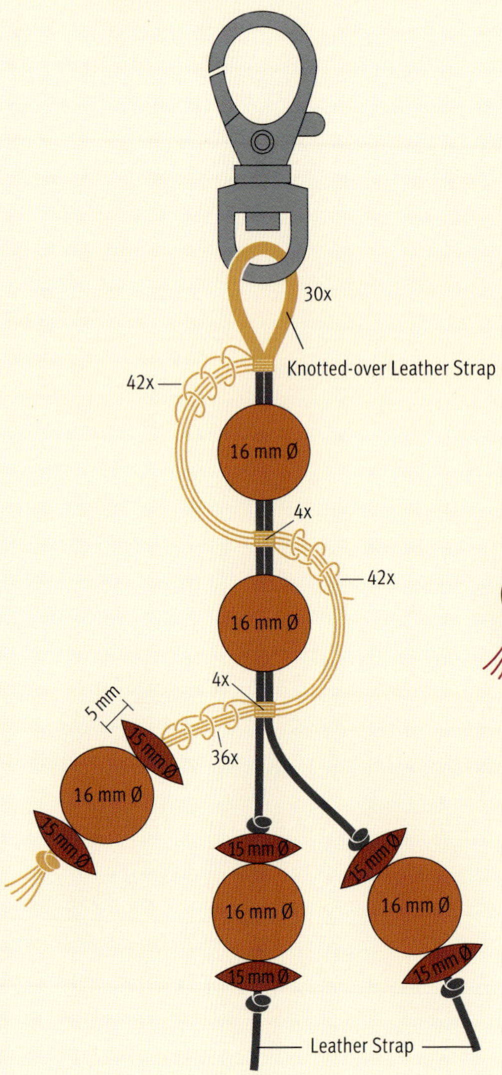

Turquoise-Blackberry

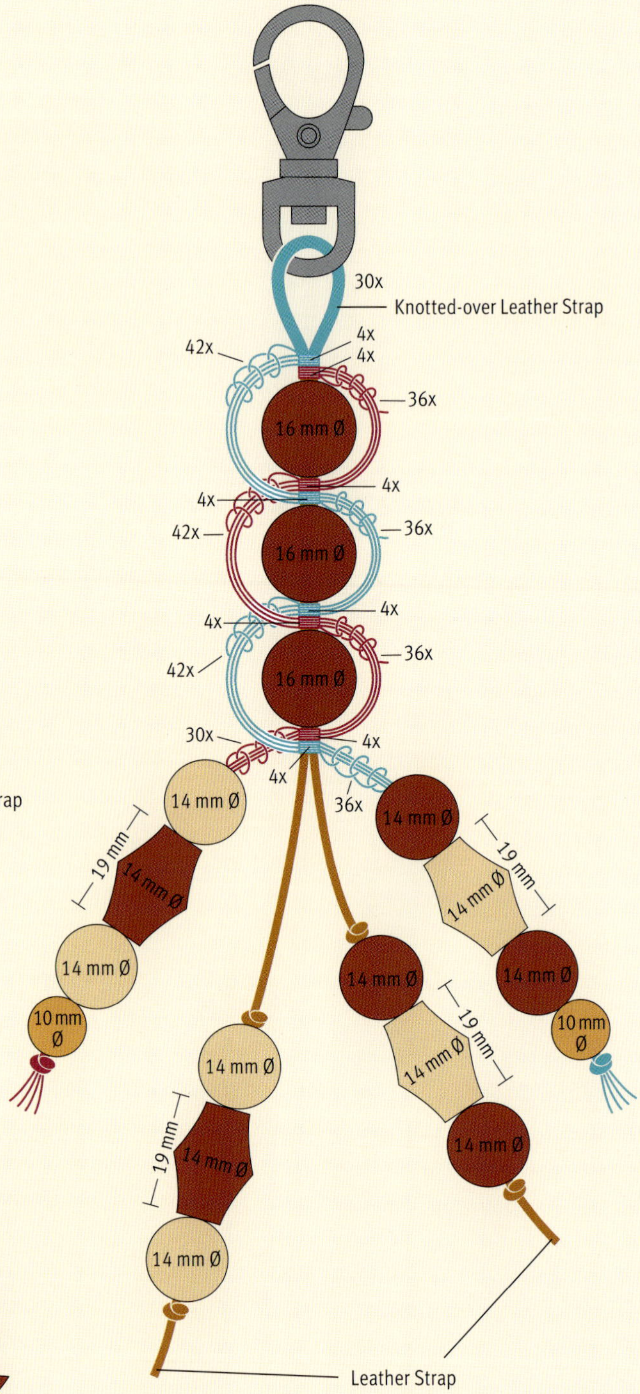

Key

Spiral knot

Thread Layout and Knotting Diagrams for “Name Bands” (Page 22)

The knotting diagram shows each entire key chain and the alphabet to create your own lettering.

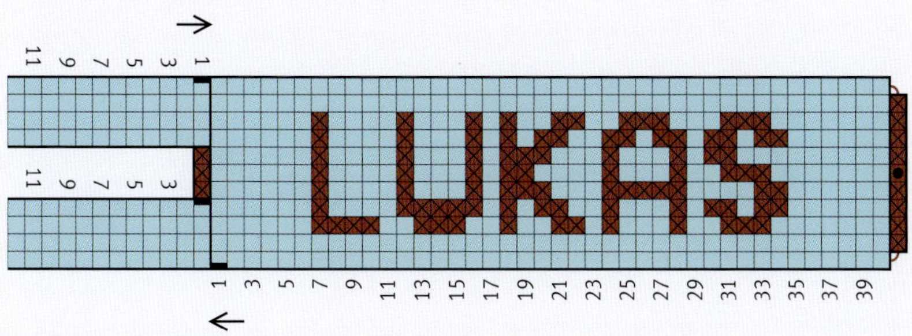

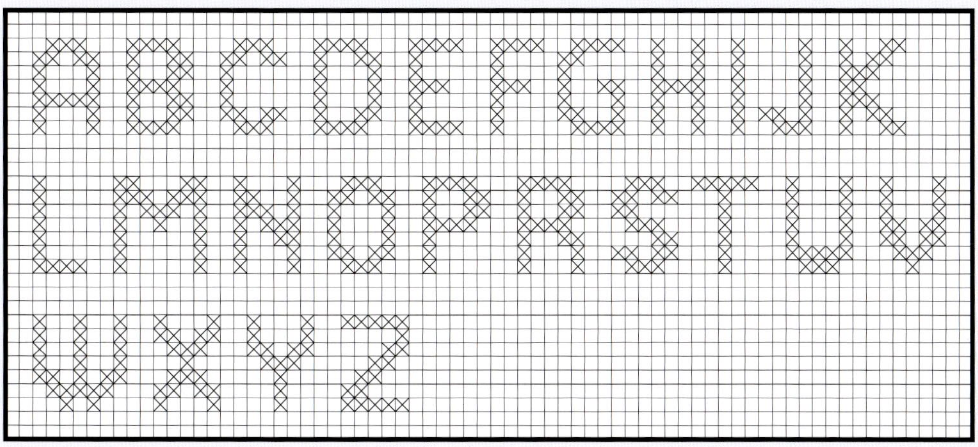

Thread Layout

Robin

- 11 core cords in green, 31 1/2 inches (80 cm) each
- Knotting cord in olive green, about 13 1/2 feet (4.10 m)
- 2 knotting cords in olive green (for the loops), 3 1/4 feet (1 m) each

Lara

- 11 core cords in pink, 27 1/2 inches (70 cm) each
- Knotting cord in blackberry, about 13 feet (4 m)
- 2 knotting cords in blackberry (for the loops), 3 1/4 feet (1 m) each

Lukas

- 11 core cords in dark brown, about 3 1/4 feet (1 m) each
- Knotting cord in turquoise, about 16 1/2 feet (5 m)
- 2 knotting cords in turquoise (for the loops), 3 1/4 feet (1 m) each

Key

↑ Direction

◧ Beginning of row

☒ Horizontal half hitch knot

☐ Vertical half hitch knot

⊡ Finishing knot

Name Bands

Materials

For All Models

- Key ring, 1 inch (25 mm) dia.

Robin

- $1^{3}/_{4}$ oz. (50 g) cotton each in green, olive-green

Lara

- $1^{3}/_{4}$ oz. (50 g) cotton each in pink, blackberry

Lukas

- $1^{3}/_{4}$ oz. (50 g) cotton each in dark brown, turquoise

Size

Robin

- $3^{3}/_{8}$ inches (8.7 cm)

Lara

- $3^{3}/_{8}$ inches (8.5 cm)

Lukas

- $3^{3}/_{4}$ inches (9.6 cm)

Thread Layout and Knotting Diagrams

Page 21

Level of Difficulty

◆◆

Robin-Band

1. Knot together the 11 core cords after approximately 8 inches (20 cm) and secure on a knotting pillow with a safety pin. Later, both loops are made over the beginning threads for attaching the key ring.

2. Begin on the left with the knotting cord and work 19 forward and 18 backward rows with vertical and horizontal half hitch knots as per the knotting diagram (basic instructions, pages 6 - 8). End the band with a final row. Release the safety pin, knot together the thread ends, and turn the band.

3. Secure the band on the knotting pillow with a safety pin. Now make both loops at the beginning of the band. For this, add one of both short knotting cords on the left and knot 6 forward and 6 backward rows over 4 core cords.

4. Make 3 horizontal half hitch knots with the core cords in green over the beginning thread of the right knotting cord between both flaps.

5. Release the safety pin, place the resulting flaps around the key ring, and tightly stitch up the thread ends on the back side. Also, stitch up the threads at the end of the band.

Tip

Create both other name bands like the Robin band, paying attention to the different row specifications in the knotting diagrams.

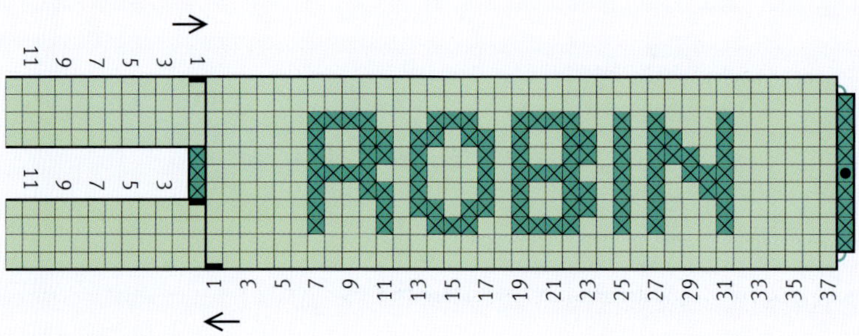

Key

- ↑ Direction
- ◧ Beginning of row
- ☒ Horizontal half hitch knot
- ☐ Vertical half hitch knot
- ◉ Finishing knot

LUKAS
LENA

Many Hearts

Materials

- $1\frac{3}{4}$ oz. (50 g) cotton each in blackberry (white) and white (black)
- White button, $\frac{3}{4}$ inches (20 mm) dia.
- Split ring, $\frac{1}{2}$ inch (14 mm) dia.
- Hair tie, $1\frac{1}{8}$ inches (30 mm) dia., approx. $\frac{1}{8}$ inch (2 mm) thick

Size

- $2\frac{1}{8}$ x $2\frac{1}{2}$ x $\frac{5}{8}$ inches (5.3 cm x 6.5 cm x 1.5 cm) (W x H x D)

Thread Layout and Knotting Diagram

Page 26

Level of Difficulty

◆◆

1. Following the basic instructions (pages 6 - 13) first make the base of the case out of 36 core cords (9 vertical threads, 27 horizontal threads). Then work the body of the case per round alternating with one of the two white (black) knotting cords offset laterally. After the 5th or 6th round stitch up the beginning threads on the inside. Continue working through round 24 according to the knotting diagram. Clip off the knotting cords and stitch up.

2. Work in both slots for the split ring on the left side of the case (basic instructions, page 11), here separating the 5 center threads for the flap between the slots. On one side of a slot, newly add a knotting cord. Work the following rows in 2 forward rows and 1 backward row according to the knotting diagram.

3. Make the flap for the split ring over the 5 threads between the slots with the other knotting cord in 3 forward and 2 backward rows. Then stitch up all beginning and ending threads on the inside. Pull the split ring on the knotted flap. Now make 5 additional rounds (28 to 32) alternating with both knotting cords.

4. For the clasp flap on the back side of the case, separate the center 29 threads and knot 12 forward and 21 backward rows (basic instructions, page 12). In the process, incorporate the hair tie with the appropriate core cord at the marked locations on the knotting diagram.

5. Lastly, knot a final row out of horizontal half hitch knots towards the center. With the remaining core cords of the side sections and the front side, also knot a final row towards the center of the front side. Finally, stitch up all threads on the inside and sew on the button.

Thread Layout and Knotting Diagram for "Many Hearts" (Page 24)

Thread Layout

For the Base and Case

- 36 core cords in blackberry (white), about 7 feet (2.20 m) each
- 2 knotting cords in white (black), about 30½ feet (9.30 m) each

For the Flap

- Knotting cord in white (black), about 19½ feet (6 m)

The knotting diagram displays the back side with the flap and both side sections. The front side and back side are identical. For a better illustration of the beginning of the rows, the knotting diagram displays a part of the front side on the left.

Key

- ↑ Direction
- ◧ Beginning of round, or rather row
- ✕ Auxiliary thread
- ⊠ Horizontal half hitch knot
- ☐ Vertical half hitch knot
- ⊡ Finishing knot
- ◎ Knotted-over hair tie
- | Include slot

Thread Layout and Knotting Diagrams for "Original Patterns" (Page 28)

The knotting diagram shows each first half of the carrying strap completely and the beginning and end from the other half. The pattern develops from the repetitions specified in the instructions.

Zigzag

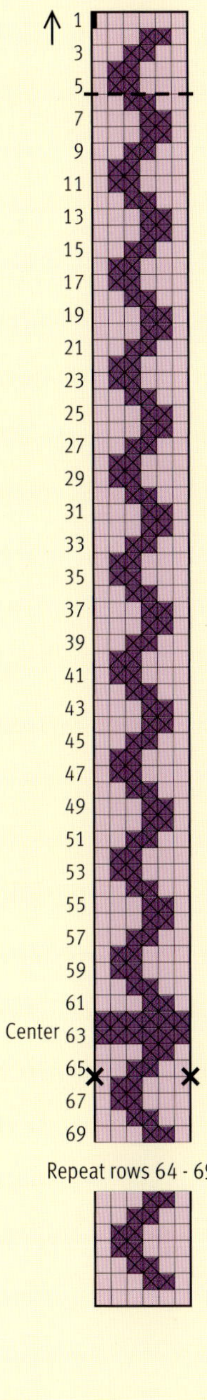

Triangle

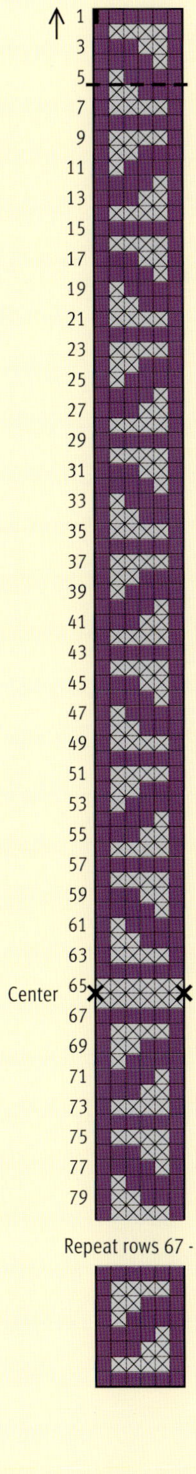

Thread Layout

Meander

- 3 core cords in green, about 11 feet (3.40 m) each
- Knotting cord in gray, about 22¼ feet (6.80 m)

Zigzag

- 3 core cords in purple, about 10 feet (3.10 m) each
- Knotting cord in pink, about 23 feet (7 m)

Triangle

- 3 core cords in gray, about 8½ feet (2.60 m) each
- Knotting cord in purple, about 23 feet (7 m)

Key

- ↑ Direction
- ◧ Beginning of row
- ⊠ Horizontal half hitch knot
- □ Vertical half hitch knot
- --- Stitch together both halves of the strap
- × Auxiliary thread for knotting the second half

Original Patterns

Materials

For All Models

- Cell phone strap, about 2 inches (5.2 cm)

Meander

- $1\frac{3}{4}$ oz. (50 g) cotton each in gray, green

Zigzag

- $1\frac{3}{4}$ oz. (50 g) cotton each in pink, purple

Triangle

- $1\frac{3}{4}$ oz. (50 g) cotton each in gray, purple

Thread Layout and Knotting Diagrams

Page 27

Sizes

Meander:

- $5\frac{3}{8}$ inches (13.7 cm)

Zigzag:

- $5\frac{1}{8}$ inches (12.9 cm)

Triangle:

- $5\frac{1}{2}$ inches (14 cm)

Level of Difficulty

◆◆

Meander Strap

1. Fold the 3 green core cords in half and put into the metal ring of the cell phone strap. Secure the loop on the knotting pillow with a safety pin.

2. Begin with the knotting cord on the left and then make 32 forward and 31 backward rows with vertical and horizontal half hitch knots as per the knotting diagram (basic instructions, pages 6 - 9). Then knot 1 forward and 1 backward row of horizontal half hitch knots.

3. Release the strap from the safety pin, turn, and now attach on the knotting pillow with an auxiliary thread and safety pin.

4. Knot back 32 forward and 31 backward rows up to the attachment loop according to the knotting diagram. Pull the thread ends through the metal ring and sew together the knotted strap to form a carrying strap.

5. Sew together both straps tightly with a short thread at the marked location on the knotting diagram so that the strap does not come apart.

Tip

Work the **zigzag** and **triangle straps** like the meander strap, however, pay attention to different row specifications in the knotting diagrams.

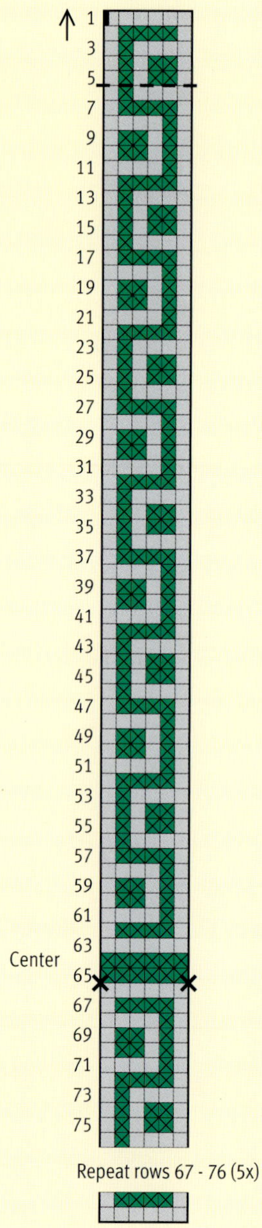

ON/OFF

Lanyards

Materials

- $1\frac{3}{4}$ oz. (50 g) cotton each in white (dark gray), rainbow colors (purple mottled pattern)
- Key chain with snap hook, 1 inch (25 mm) dia.

Thread Layout

- 5 core cords in white (dark gray), about 10 feet (3 m) each
- 2 knotting cords in white (dark gray) for the beginning and end of the strap, about $6\frac{1}{2}$ feet (2 m) each
- 6 knotting cords in white (dark gray), about $5\frac{1}{4}$ feet (1.60 m) each
- 17 knotting cords in rainbow colors (purple mottled pattern), about $5\frac{1}{4}$ feet (1.60 m) each

Size

- $17\frac{7}{8}$ inches (45.5 cm)

Level of Difficulty

◆◆

Rainbow Strap

1. Fold the 5 threads in half and hang in the snap hook. Start with the longer knotting cord on the left for the beginning and work 5 forward and 4 backward rows with vertical half hitch knots according to the knotting diagram, combining several threads in the process.

2. Turn the strap and knot 5 forward and 5 backward rows according to the knotting diagram. In the process, add a different colored thread at the marked location.

3. Stitch up the beginning and ending threads on the back side. Slightly pull on both outer core cords so that the strap easily bends. Continue making the following rows according to the knotting diagram. Turn the strap at each specified location.

4. Pull the thread ends through the snap hook; tightly stitch together the beginning and end of the strap, stitch up and clip off the threads.

Tip

Make the lanyard in purple-gray according to the same pattern as the strap in rainbow colors.

The knotting diagram shows the beginning and end of the strap. The pattern develops from the repetitions that are specified in the instructions.

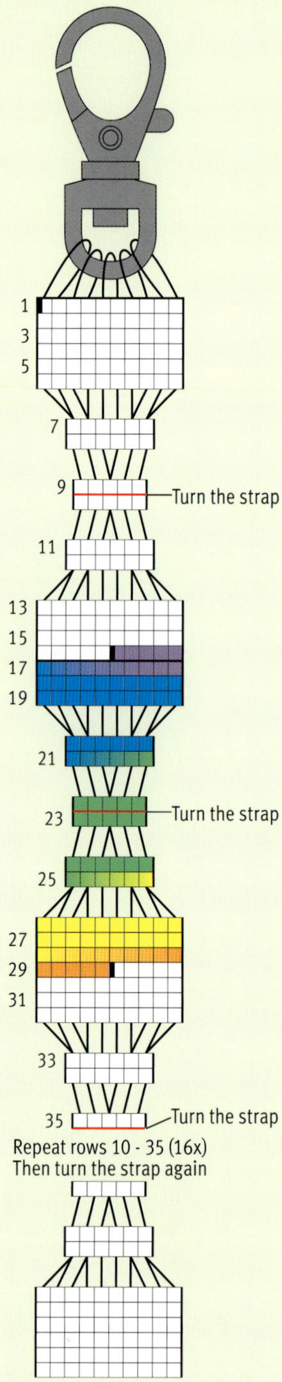

Key

↑ Direction

□ Vertical half hitch knot

◧ Change the thread color (add a new thread)

Cell Phone Cases

Materials

- $1\frac{3}{4}$ oz. (50 g) cotton each in dark blue (beige), turquoise (blackberry/pink)
- Wooden toggle button, $1\frac{1}{8}$ inches (3 cm)

Thread Layout and Knotting Diagram

Page 34

Size

- $1\frac{7}{8}$ x 4 x $\frac{7}{8}$ inches (4.8 cm x 10 cm x 2.2 cm) (W x H x D)

Level of Difficulty

◆◆

1. According to the basic instructions (pages 6 - 13), first make the base of the case out of 36 core cords (12 vertical threads, 24 horizontal threads).

2. Now work the case per round alternating with one of the two knotting cords in turquoise (blackberry) offset laterally.

3. After the 5th or 6th round stitch up the beginning threads on the inside. Continue working through round 48 according to the knotting diagram.

4. For the case variation in beige and red tones switch the knotting cords after 12 rounds. Stitch up the knotting cords.

5. For the clasp flap on the back side of the case, separate the center 26 threads and knot 16 forward and 15 backward rows. Lastly, knot a final row of horizontal half hitch knots towards the center.

6. Make the loop on the end of the flap with 48 spiral knots (basic instructions, page 8). Tightly stitch up the thread ends on the inside.

7. With the remaining core cords of the side sections and the front side also knot a final row towards the center of the front side.

8. Finally, clip off all threads, stitch up on the inside, and sew on the toggle button on the front side.

Thread Layout and Knotting Diagram for "Cell Phone Cases" (Page 32)

Thread Layout

Case in Blue and Turquoise

For the Base and Case

- 36 core cords in dark blue, about 10 feet (3 m) each
- 2 knotting cords in turquoise, about 41 feet (12.50 m) each

For the Flap

- Knotting cord in turquoise, about 10 feet (3.10 m)

Case in Beige & Red Tones

For the Base and Case

- 36 core cords in beige, about 10 feet (3 m) each
- 2 knotting cords in blackberry, about 10½ feet (3.20 m) each
- 2 knotting cords in pink, about 10½ feet (3.20 m) each

For the Flap

- Knotting cord in blackberry, about 10 feet (3.10 m)

Key

- ↑ Direction
- ◧ Beginning of round, or rather row
- × Auxiliary thread
- ⊠ Horizontal half hitch knot
- ☐ Vertical half hitch knot
- ⊡ A Finishing knot
- Spiral knot

The knotting diagram shows the base, the back side with the case flap, and the side sections. The front and back sides are identical.

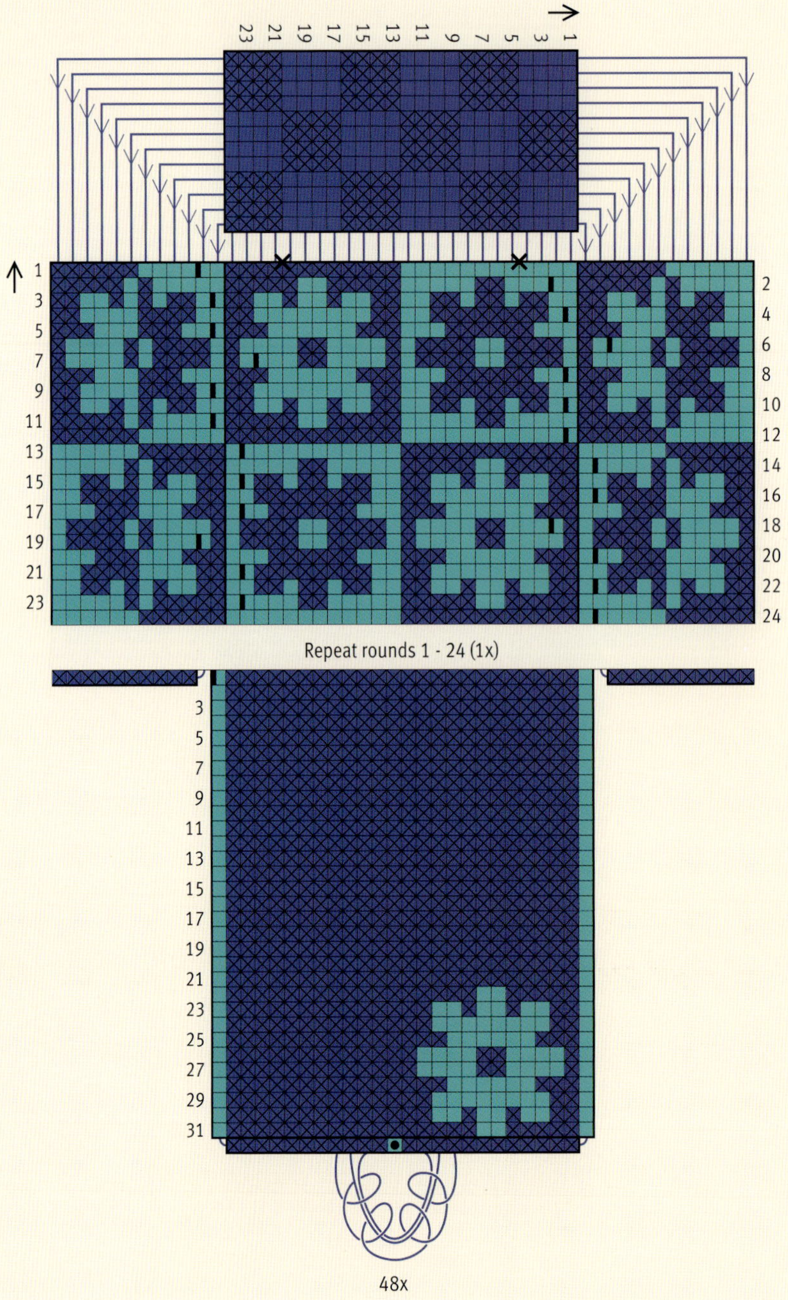

Thread Layout and Knotting Diagram for "Eyeglasses Case" (Page 36)

The knotting diagram shows the bottom half, the back side with the case flap, and half of the side section. The front and back sides, as well as the other halves of the side sections, are identical.

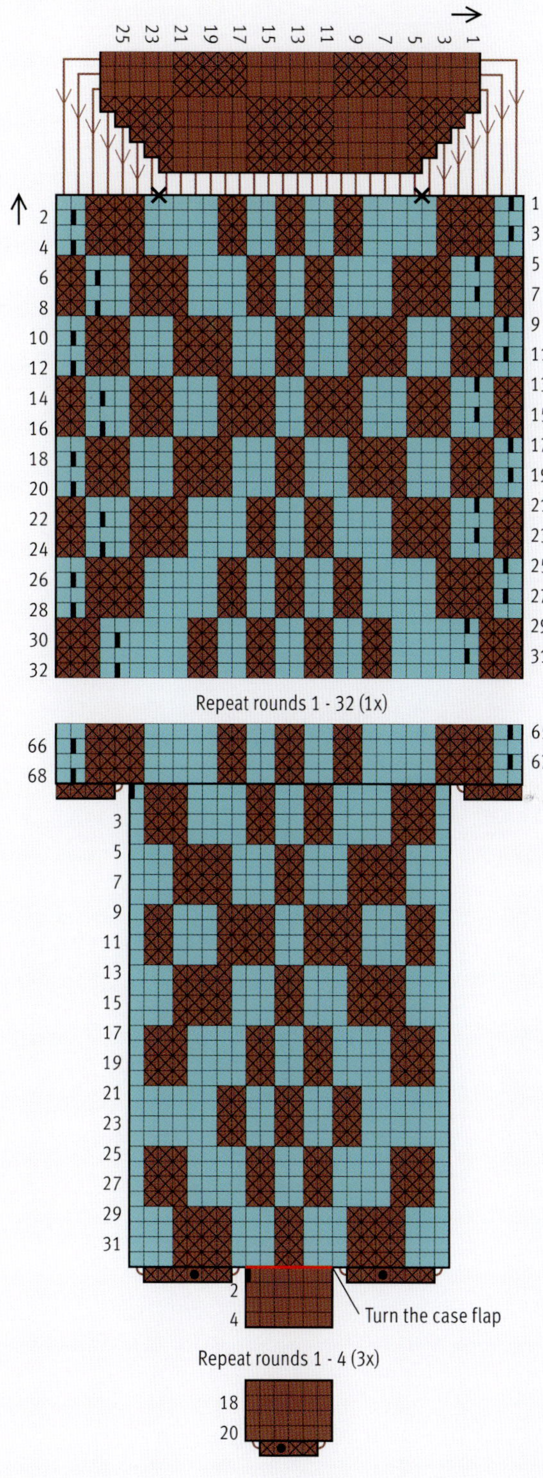

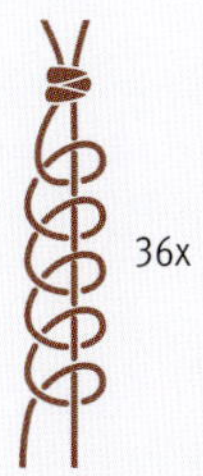

Detail illustration of the clasp loop on the front side.

Thread layout

For the Base and Case

- 42 core cords in dark brown (pink), about 8 feet (2.50 m) each
- 2 knotting cords in turquoise (dark brown), about 54 feet (16.4 m) each

For the Flap

- Knotting cord in turquoise (dark brown), about 19 feet (5.8 m)

For the Clasp Flap

- Knotting cord in dark brown (pink), about $6^1/_2$ feet (2 m)

For the Clasp Loop

- 2 knotting cords in dark brown (pink), about $6^1/_2$ feet (2 m) each

Key

- ↑ Direction
- Beginning of round, or rather row
- × Auxiliary thread
- ☒ Horizontal half hitch
- ☐ Vertical half hitch knot
- Finishing knot
- Spiral knot

Eyeglasses Case

Materials
- $1^3/_4$ oz. (50 g) cotton each in dark brown (pink), turquoise (dark brown)
- Clasp (hook and eye; PRYM-No.2 shown here)

Thread Layout and Knotting Diagram
Page 35

Size
- 2 x $5^3/_4$ x 1 inches (5 cm x 14.7 cm x 2.6 cm) (W x H x D)

Level of Difficulty
◆◆◆

1. According to the basic instructions (pages 6 - 13) first make the base of the case from 42 core cords (16 vertical threads, 26 horizontal threads). Now work the case per round, alternating with one of both turquoise-colored (dark-brown colored) knotting cords offset laterally. Because the base of the case for this model is round, several threads in the 1st round are omitted and stitched up on the inside (see knotting diagram). After the 5th or 6th round also stitch up the beginning threads on the inside.

2. Continue working through round 50 according to the knotting pattern. Now, separately knot a clasp loop: Here make 36 spiral knots with both threads. Stitch the thread ends on the front side of the case after the 47th and 48th round (later the case is too high). Work 18 additional rounds alternating with both knotting cords. Clip off the knotting cords and stitch up.

3. For the clasp flap, separate the center 22 threads on the back side of the case (basic instructions, page 12) and knot 16 forward and 16 backward rows. Turn the case flap and again separate the center 6 threads for the flap and work 10 forward and 10 backward rows. End the flap with a final row. Make two final rows on the left and right of the flap. With the remaining core cords of the side sections and the front side also knot a final row towards the center.

4. Finally, clip off all threads, stitch up on the inside, and sew on an "eye" at the end of the flap at a distance of approximately 1 inch (2.5 cm) and a hook on the flap (see detailed view). To close the case pull the flap under the clasp loop and hook on the flap.

Pen Covers

Materials

- $1\frac{3}{4}$ oz. (50 g) cotton each in white (orange) or brown/turquoise
- Black fine liner pen (i.e., Stabilo point 88)
- Fabric glue (HT2 recommended)
- 64 cube-shaped Rocaille beads in different colors (orange or blue tones), $\frac{1}{8}$ inch (4 mm)
- Needle to thread on the beads

Thread Layout and Knotting Diagram

Page 40

Size

- Approximately $6\frac{3}{4}$ inches (17 cm)

Level of Difficulty

◆◆

1. For the pen covers, fold the 8 core cords in half and tie together in the center with a short, same-colored thread – approximately 2 inches (5 cm) long. In the first round, make 8 horizontal half hitch knots over the knotting cord (see knotting diagram); at the same time evenly spreading out the knots on both sides of the center. It is helpful to mark the 1st beginning thread or round with a knot.

2. In the 2nd round, also incorporate the remaining core cords. After the 2nd round, bring in the auxiliary thread, knot together, and secure on a knotting pillow with a safety pin.

3. Now, continue knotting according to the pattern. Thread on a rectangular bead on 2 core cords at the marked location. In the following 2 rounds, take the knotting cord through under the beads and knot two vertical half hitch knots at the appropriate location (marked on the knotting diagram).

4. After the 7th round, put the pen into the cover that has already been knotted. Continue working according to the pattern. After the 69th round clip off the threads except for $\frac{3}{8}$ inch (1 cm) and place into the cover.

5. Work the cover for the cap just the same as the cover for the pen, however, only knot 19 rounds. After approximately 5 rounds, pull this cover onto the pen cap.

6. Finally, clip off all threads except for $\frac{3}{8}$ inch (1 cm) and place inward. Attach the shorter cover with fabric glue on the pen cap. Do not glue the other cover so that the pen can be switched out.

Thread Layout and Knotting Diagram for "Pen Covers" (Page 38)

Thread Layout

For the Pen Cover

- 8 core cords in white (orange or turquoise), about $6^{1}/_{2}$ feet (2 m) each
- Knotting cord in white (orange or brown), about $24^{1}/_{2}$ feet (7.50 m)

For the Pen Cap

- 8 core cords in white (orange or turquoise), $19^{5}/_{8}$ inches (50 cm) each
- Knotting cord in white (orange or brown), about $6^{1}/_{2}$ feet (2 m)

The knotting diagram shows the cover for the pen and for the pen cap.

Pen Cover

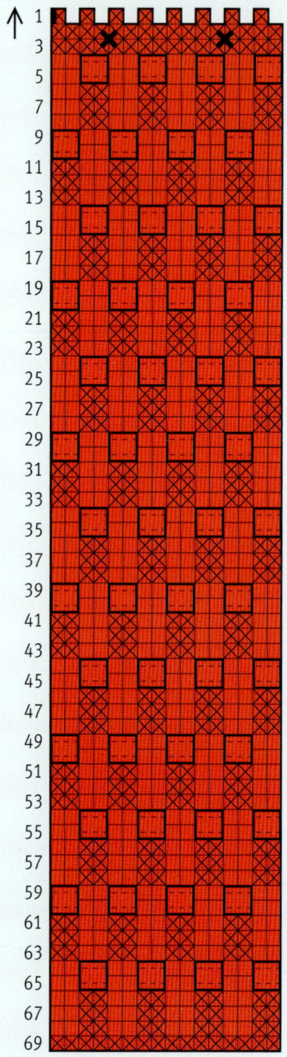

Pen Cap

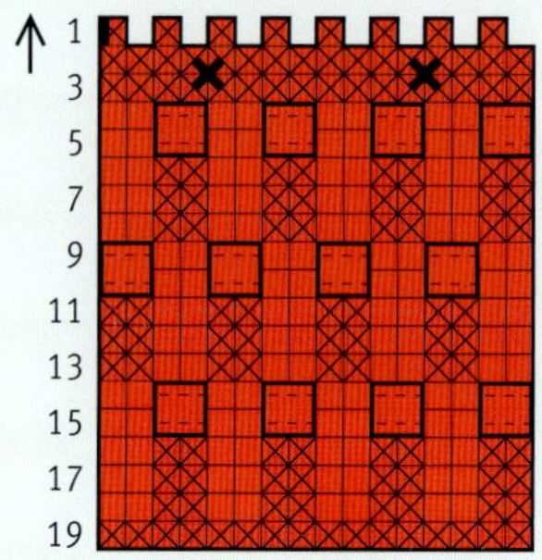

Key

- ↑ Direction
- Beginning of round
- × Auxiliary thread
- ⊠ Horizontal half hitch knot
- □ Vertical half hitch knot
- Rectangular beads
- - - - At these locations the knotting cord is placed along under the beads and incorporated again after the bead.

Thread Layout and Knotting Diagrams for “Fine Rose” (Page 42)

The knotting diagram shows the base, the back side with the case flap, and the side sections of the little case. The front and back sides are identical. Additionally, the beginning and the end of the strap is illustrated. The pattern develops from the repetitions specified in the instructions.

Cell Phone Case

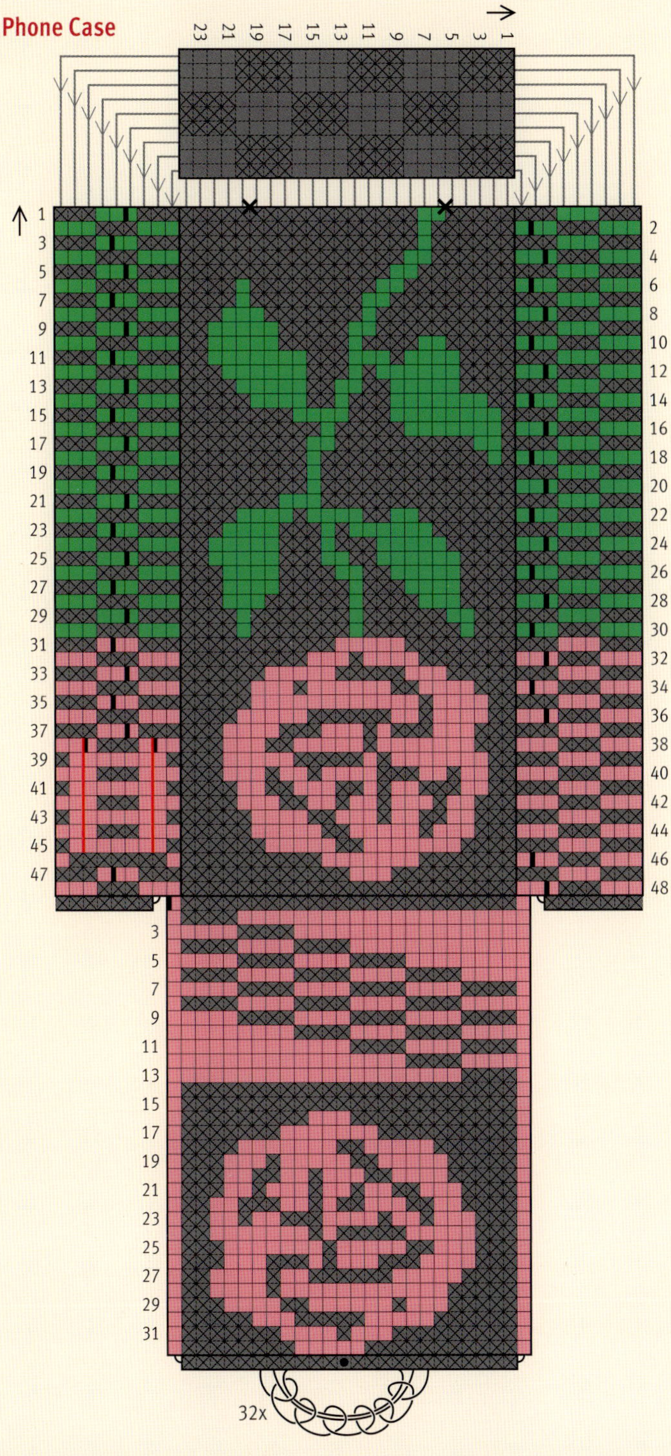

Lanyard

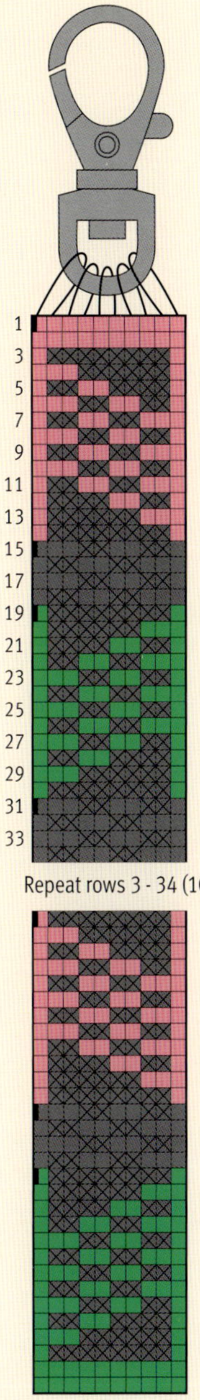

Thread Layout Little Rose Case

For the Base and Case

- 33 core cords in black, about 10 feet (3 m) each
- 2 knotting cords in green, about 21 feet (6.50 m) each
- 2 knotting cords in rose-pink mottled pattern, about 20 1/2 feet (6.3 m) each (for the blossom)

For the Flap

- Knotting cord in rose-pink mottled pattern, about 14 3/4 feet (4.50 m)

Lanyard

- 5 core cords in black, about 31 feet (9.50 m) long each
- 11 knotting cords in rose-pink mottled pattern, about 4 feet (1.20 m) each
- Knotting cord in rose-pink mottled pattern (for the beginning), about 6 feet (1.80 m)
- 11 knotting cords in green, about 4 feet (1.20 m) each
- Knotting cord in green (for the end), about 6 feet (1.8 m)
- 23 knotting cords in black, 35 1/2 inches (90 cm) each

Key

- ↑ Direction
- ◧ Beginning of round, or rather row
- × Auxiliary thread
- ☒ Horizontal half hitch knot
- ☐ Vertical half hitch knot
- ⊡ Finishing knot
- Spiral knot
- | Include slot

Fine Rose

Materials

Rose Case

- $1\frac{3}{4}$ oz. (50 g) cotton each in black, green, rose-pink mottled pattern
- Black button, $\frac{1}{2}$ inch (14 mm) dia.
- Split ring, $\frac{1}{2}$ inch (14 mm) dia.

Lanyard

- $1\frac{3}{4}$ oz. (50 g) cotton each in black, green, pink-rose mottled pattern
- Key chain with snap hook, 1 inch (25 mm dia.)

Thread Layout and Knotting Diagrams

Page 41

Sizes

Case:

- 2 x $4\frac{1}{8}$ x $\frac{3}{4}$ inches (5 cm x 10.6 cm x 2 cm) (W x H x D)

Strap:

- 17 inches (43 cm)

Level of Difficulty

Case ◆◆

Strap ◆

Rose Case

1. According to the basic instructions (pages 6 - 13), first make the base of the case from 33 core cords (9 vertical threads, 24 horizontal threads). Now work the case per round alternating with one of the two green knotting cords offset laterally. After the 5th or 6th round stitch up the beginning threads on the inside. Continue working through round 30 as per the knotting diagram. Stitch up the green knotting cords. Add the pink mottled knotting cords and continue knotting through round 37.

2. Work in both slots for the split ring on the left side of the case from round 38, here separating the center 5 threads for the flap between the slots. Newly add a knotting cord on one side of a slot. Work the following rows in 4 forward and 4 backward rows according to the knotting diagram. Knot the flap for the split ring over the 5 threads between the slots with the other knotting cord in 4 forward and 4 backward rows. Then stitch up all beginning and ending threads on the inside. Pull the split ring on the knotted flap. Make three additional rounds alternating with both knotting cords.

3. For the clasp flap on the back side of the case, separate the 26 center threads (basic instructions, page 12), and knot 16 forward and 16 backward rows, then work a final row. Make the loop on the end of the flap (basic instructions, page 12) with 32 spiral knots. Stitch up the thread ends on the inside. With the remaining core cords of the side sections and the front side also knot a final row. Stitch up all threads and attach the button.

Lanyard

Fold the 5 threads in half and hang into the snap hook. As per the knotting diagram, make the lanyard in forward and backward rows, making sure to switch the color of the knotting cord at the marked locations. Then stitch up all beginning and ending threads on the back side. Pull the thread ends of the core cords through the snap hook, tightly stitch together the beginning and the end of the strap, and clip off the threads.

Handbag

Materials

- 9 oz. (250 g) cotton blend thread (55% cotton, 45% polyacrylic) in blackberry (length 279 feet [or 85 m] / $1^3/_4$ oz. [or 50 g])
- 3 ½ oz. (100 g) cotton blend thread in light green (length about 279 feet or 85 m / 1 $^3/_4$ oz. or 50 g)
- 2 buttons in blackberry, $^7/_8$ inches (23 mm) dia.

Thread Layout and Knotting Diagram

Page 46

Size

- $6^3/_4$ x $6^1/_8$ x 1 inches (17 cm x 15.5 cm x 2.5 cm) (W x H x D)

Level of Difficulty

◆◆

1. According to the basic instructions (pages 6 - 13), first make the base of the bag from 61 core cords in blackberry (8 vertical threads, 53 horizontal threads). Now work the bag per round alternating with one of the two light green knotting cords offset laterally. After the 5th or 6th round stitch up the beginning threads on the inside. As per the knotting diagram, continue working through round 48 and stitch up the knotting cords.

2. For the clasp flap on the back side of the bag, separate the center 55 threads (basic instructions, page 12) and knot 12 forward and 12 backward rows.

3. In rows 25 to 31, work in both button holes. For this, first knot the left side section in 4 forward and 3 backward rows over 13 core cords. Newly add the knotting cord and work the section between the button holes in 4 forward and 3 backward rows. Then newly add the knotting cord for the right side section (see knotting diagram) and make 4 forward and 3 backward rows.

4. Add the knotting cord to the left again and completely knot 1 forward and 1 backward row. Lastly, make a final row out of horizontal half hitch knots towards the center.

5. With the remaining core cords of the side sections and the front side, also knot a final row towards the center of the front side. Finally, clip off all threads, stitch up on the inside, and sew both buttons on the front side.

6. For the strap, knot together 12 threads in blackberry and secure on a knotting pillow with a safety pin. Separate the 12 threads into 4 strands, 3 threads each, and make 145 square knots (instructions, page 8). After 10 square knots always turn the inner strands outwards to continue knotting with these. Thus, the threads will be equally used. Tightly stitch on the finished strap inside on the side of the bag.

Thread Layout and Knotting Diagram for "Handbag" (Page 44)

Thread Layout

For the Base and Bag

- 61 core cords in blackberry, about 17 feet (5.20 m) each
- 2 knotting cords in light green, about 115 feet (35 m) each

For the Flap

- Knotting cord in light green, about 55¾ feet (17 m)

For the Strap

- 12 threads in blackberry, about 16½ feet (5 m) each

The knotting diagram shows the base, the back side with the case flap, and the side sections. The front and back sides are identical.

Key

- ↑ Direction
- ◧ Beginning of round, or rather row
- × Auxiliary thread
- ⊠ Horizontal half hitch knot
- □ Vertical half hitch knot
- ⊡ Finishing knot
- | Include slot

Thread Layout and Knotting Diagram for "Lighter Cases" (Page 48)

The knotting diagram shows the base, the back side with the case flap, the side sections, and the front section.

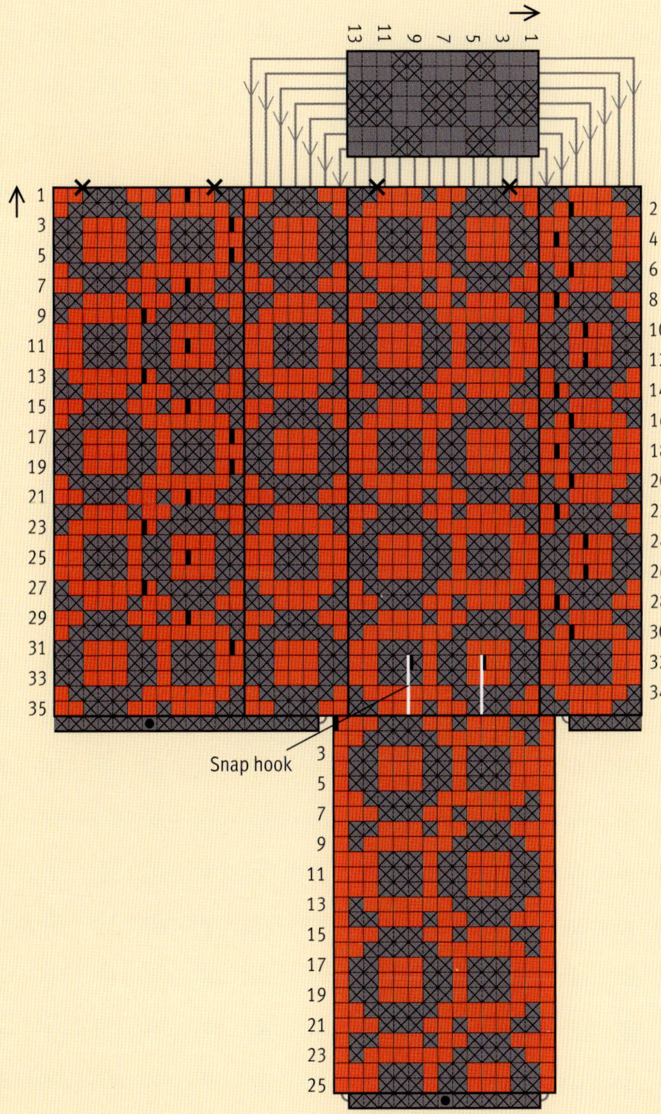

Thread Layout

For the Base and Case

- 20 core cords in beige (gray), about 6½ feet (2 m) each
- 2 knotting cords in dark blue (dark orange), about 21 feet (6.4 m) each

For the Flap

- Knotting cord in dark blue (dark orange), about 11 feet (3.5 m)

Key

- ↑ Direction
- ◧ Beginning of round, or rather row
- × Auxiliary thread
- ☒ Horizontal half hitch knot
- ☐ Vertical half hitch knot
- ⊡ Finishing knot
- | Include slot

Lighter Cases

Materials

- $1^{3}/_{4}$ oz. (50 g) cotton each in beige (gray), dark blue (orange)
- Snap fastener "color" in black or dark blue, $^{1}/_{2}$ inch (13 mm) dia.
- Snap hook with an attached eye, approximately $2^{3}/_{4}$ inches (7 cm)

Thread Layout and Knotting Diagram

Page 47

Size

- 1 x 3 x $^{1}/_{2}$ inches (2.6 cm x 7.6 cm x 1.2 cm) (W x H x D)

Level of Difficulty

◆◆

1. According to the basic instructions (pages 6 - 13), first make the base of the case from 20 core cords (7 vertical threads, 13 horizontal threads). Now work the case per round alternating with one of the two dark blue (orange-colored) knotting cords offset laterally. After the 5th or 6th round, stitch up the beginning threads on the inside. Continue working through round 31 as per the knotting pattern. Stitch up the knotting cords

2. Work in both slots for the snap hook on the back side of the case starting from round 32 (basic instructions, page 11), here separating the center 5 threads for the flap between the slots. On one side of a slot, newly add a knotting cord. Work the following rows according to the knotting pattern. Knot the flap for the split ring over the 5 threads between the slots with the other knotting cord. Then stitch up all beginning and ending threads on the inside. Pull the split ring on the knotted flap.

3. For the clasp flap on the back side of the case, separate the center 15 threads (basic instructions, page 12) and knot 13 forward and 12 backward rows. Then work a final row and stitch up the thread ends on the inside. With the remaining core cords of the side sections and the front section also knot a final row and stitch up all threads. Attach the snap fastener.

Modern Colors

Materials

- $1^{3}/_{4}$ oz. (50 g) cotton each in turquoise (dark orange), dark brown (yellow), light brown (turquoise)
- White side release buckle, $^{3}/_{8}$ inch (10 mm) wide
- Split ring, $^{1}/_{2}$ inch (14 mm) dia.

Thread Layout and Knotting Diagram

Page 52

Size

- $2^{1}/_{8}$ x 4 x 1 inches (5.5 cm x 10.2 cm x 2.4 cm) (W x H x D)

Level of Difficulty

◆◆

1. According to the basic instructions (pages 6 - 13), first make the base of the case from 40 core cords (13 vertical threads, 27 horizontal threads). Now work the case per round alternating with both dark brown (yellow) knotting cords offset laterally. After the 5th or 6th round, stitch up the beginning threads on the inside. As per the knotting diagram, continue working through round 40.

2. Work in both slots for the split ring on the right side of the case (basic instructions, page 11), here separating the center 3 threads for the flap between the slots. On one side of a slot newly add a knotting cord (see knotting diagram). Work the following rows in 2 forward rows and 1 backward row as per the knotting pattern.

3. Knot the flap for the split ring over the 3 threads between the slots with the other knotting cord in 3 forward and 2 backward rows. Then stitch up all beginning and ending threads on the inside. Pull the split ring on the knotted flap. With both knotting cords, make 5 additional rounds alternating according to the pattern.

4. For the clasp flap on the back side of the case separate the center 29 threads (basic instructions, page 12) and knot 14 forward and 13 backward rows.

5. On the end of the flap, separate the center 5 threads for the flap and knot 6 forward and 6 backward rows. Afterwards, with the threads of this narrow flap sew on one piece of the side release buckle. Work 2 final rows on the left and right of the flap.

6. With the remaining core cords of the side sections and the front side knot a final row towards the center of the front side. Finally, stitch up all threads on the inside. Sew on the other piece of the side release buckle on the front side of the case.

Thread Layout and Knotting Diagram for "Modern Colors" (Page 50)

(Page 50)

Thread Layout

For the Base and Case

- 40 core cords in turquoise (dark orange), about 8 feet (2.5 m) each
- 4 knotting cords in dark brown (yellow), about 20 feet (6.2 m) each
- 2 knotting cords in light brown (turquoise), about 9 feet (2.8 m) each

For the Flap

- Knotting cord in light brown (turquoise), about 7 feet (2.2 m)
- Knotting cord in dark brown (yellow), about 12½ feet (3.8 m)

For the Flap

- Knotting cord in turquoise (orange), about 3¼ feet (1 m)

The knotting diagram shows the base, the back side with the case flap and the side sections. The front and back sides are identical.

Key

- Direction
- Beginning of round, or rather row
- Auxiliary thread
- Horizontal half hitch knot
- Vertical half hitch knot
- Finishing knot
- Include slot

Thread Layout and Knotting Diagram for "Pencil Case" (Page 54)

Thread Layout

For the Base and Case

- 24 core cords each in pink, brown, about 18 feet (5.4 m)
- 2 knotting cords each in pink, brown, about 131 feet (40 m)

For the Flap

- 7 core cords each in pink, brown, about 4 feet (1.2 m)

The knotting diagram shows both round side sections as well as the main section of the case. The second side section (end) is knotted in two halves and stitched together in the center.

Detailed illustration of the 2nd side section (end) that shows which threads are not incorporated.

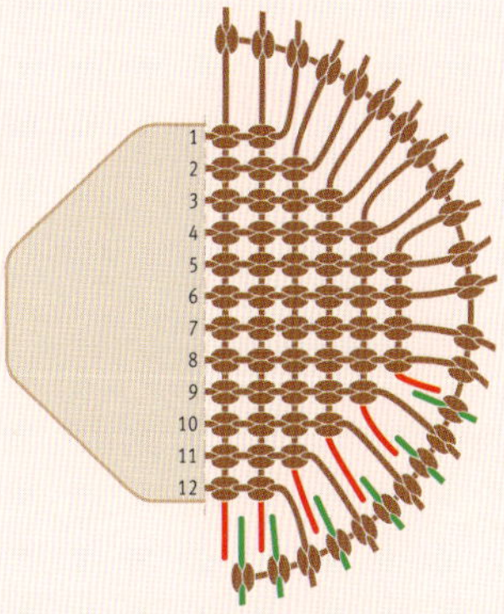

Key

- ↑ Direction
- ◧ Beginning of row
- ✕ Auxiliary thread
- ☒ Horizontal half hitch
- ☐ Vertical half hitch knot
- ⊡ Knot on a separate thread on each side of the finishing knots
- ✱ Omit these threads when knotting the 2nd side section and later stitch up on the inside.
- = Omit these threads, place inward, and later stitch up on the inside

Pencil Case

Materials

- $3^{1}/_{2}$ oz. (100 g) cotton in pink (length about 410 feet [or 125 m] / $1^{3}/_{4}$ oz. [50 g])
- 7 oz. (200) blended thread in brown (length about 213 feet [or 65 m] / $1^{3}/_{4}$ oz. (50 g)
- 2 silver clasps for opening, $1\ ^{3}/_{8}$ inches (35 mm)

Thread Layout and Knotting Diagram

Page 53

Size

- $8^{1}/_{4}$ inches (21 cm) long

Level of Difficulty

◆◆◆

1. This model is worked with doubled threads (core cords and knotting cords), thus the weave will be very stable. To begin, make the first side section from 24 doubled core cords (12 vertical threads, 12 horizontal threads) (basic instructions, pages 6 - 13). In the process, knot 4 vertical half hitch knots over 4 vertical threads in the first row. In the following rows add a thread to each left and right side and also knot over with vertical half hitch knots.

2. In the following rows, continue including a thread to the left and right each until all 12 core cords are knotted in. To obtain a nice curve knot, a round of horizontal half hitch knots over a short doubled thread approximately $19^{5}/_{8}$ inches (50 cm) and end with a finishing knot.

3. Secure the side section on the knotting pillow with auxiliary threads and a safety pin. Add the doubled knotting cord on the left and make 25 forward and 25 backward rows as per the knotting diagram, at the end of the 1st row, knot on the 7 additional core cords for the clasp flap with horizontal half hitch knots.

4. After the 50th row, repeatedly work a round with horizontal half hitch knots over another doubled, short thread, approximately $19\ ^{5}/_{8}$ inches (50 cm) and end this round with a finishing knot.

5. Make the second side section in two halves towards the center, omitting several threads and later stitching up on the inside (see detailed illustration page 53).

6. Turn the case inside out and stitch up the vertical slot in the center of the side section with the thread ends crosswise on the inside. Also stitch up all other threads on the inside. Sew on two clasps for opening.

Case With a Mirror

Materials

- $1^{3}/_{4}$ oz. (50 g) cotton each in olive green (pink), green (purple)
- Button, $^{1}/_{2}$ inches (15 mm) dia.
- Split ring, $^{5}/_{8}$ inches (14 mm) dia.
- Split ring with chain, 1 inch (25 mm) dia.
- Hair tie, $1^{1}/_{8}$ inch (30 mm dia.), approx. $^{1}/_{8}$ inch (2 mm) thick
- Mirror, $19^{5}/_{8}$ x $19^{5}/_{8}$ inches (50 cm x 50 cm)

Thread Layout and Knotting Diagram

Page 58

Size

- $2^{1}/_{2}$ x $3^{1}/_{8}$ x $^{1}/_{2}$ inches (6.5 cm x 8 cm x 1.2 cm) (W x H x D)

Level of Difficulty

◆◆◆

1. According to the basic instructions (pages 6 - 13), first make the base of the case from 39 core cords (7 vertical threads, 32 horizontal threads). Now work the case per round alternating with one of the two green (purple-colored) knotting cords offset laterally. After the 5th or 6th round, stitch up the beginning threads on the inside. Continue working through round 31 according to the knotting pattern. Clip off the knotting cords and stitch up.

2. On the right side of the case work in both slots for the split ring (basic instructions, page 11), here separating the center 3 threads for the flap between the slots. On one side of a slot newly add a knotting cord. Work the following rows in 2 forward rows and 1 backward row according to the knotting diagram. Work the flap for the split ring over the 3 threads between the slots with the other knotting cord in 3 forward and 3 backward rows. Then stitch up all beginning and ending threads on the inside. Pull the split ring on the knotted flap. Now make 3 additional rounds alternating with both knotting cords.

3. For the clasp flap on the back side of the case, separate the center 34 threads and knot 22 forward and 22 backward rows (basic instructions, page 12). At the same time, incorporate the elastic band at the marked locations. Then make a final row towards the center. With the remaining core cords of the side sections and the front side also knot a final row towards the center of the front side. Finally, stitch up and clip off all threads on the inside and sew on the button on the bottom of the back side of the case.

4. For the mirror frame, knot the 32 core cords on the short thread (27 $^{1}/_{2}$ inches or 70 cm) with horizontal half hitch knots. Secure the short thread on the knotting pillow with a safety pin. Add the knotting cord to the left for the top and left border. After the 6th row, knot over only the 7 left core cords (until row 24). Add the knotting cord for the right border and work 9 forward and 9 backward rows over the 7 right threads as per the knotting diagram. Cut off the center 18 threads after approximately 4 inches (10 cm). For the bottom border, add the knotting cord to the far left and make 4 forward and 3 backward rows, incorporating the clipped-off threads here again with horizontal half hitch knots. Stitch up the beginning and ending threads on the back side. Stitch down the finished frame with a green thread on the marked location on the front side of the case, insert the mirror before the last side is stitched shut.

Frame for the Mirror

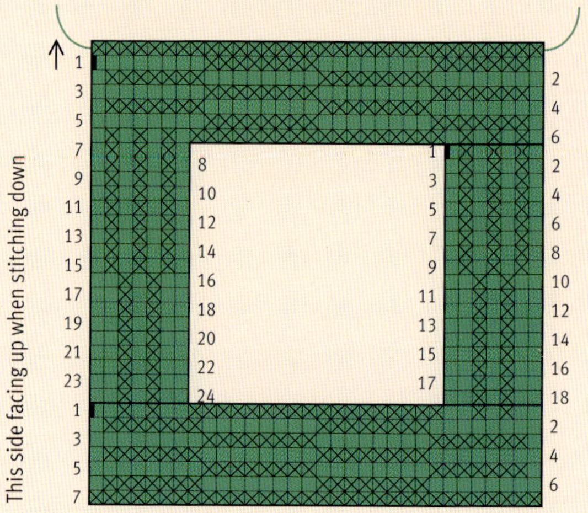

Key

- ↑ Direction
- ◧ Beginning of row
- ☒ Horizontal half hitch knot
- ☐ Vertical half hitch knot

MACpraxis
Gute
Apples Adressbuch wirkt auf den ersten Blick übersichtlich.
KONTAKTE ZUSAM

Thread Layout and Knotting Diagram for "Case With A Mirror" (Page 56)

Thread Layout

For the Base and Case

- 39 core cords in olive green (pink), about 6½ feet (2 m) each
- 2 knotting cords in green (purple), about 43¼ feet (13.20 m) each

For the Flap

- Knotting cord in green (purple), 41 feet (12.50 m)

For the Knotted Frame in Green (Purple)

- 32 core cords, about 3 feet (1 m) each
- Core cord for the first row (beginning), 27½ inches (70 cm)
- Knotting cord for the top and left border, about 10 feet (3 m)
- Knotting cord for the right border, about 4½ feet (1.4 m)
- Knotting cord for the bottom border, about 5½ feet (1.70 m)

Key

- ↑ Direction
- Beginning of round, or rather row
- × Auxiliary thread
- ☒ Horizontal half hitch knot
- ☐ Vertical half hitch knot
- ● Finishing knot
- ◎ Include the elastic band at this location
- At this location the frame is stitched down on the front side

The knotting diagram shows the base, the back side with the flap, and both side sections. The front side and back side are identical.

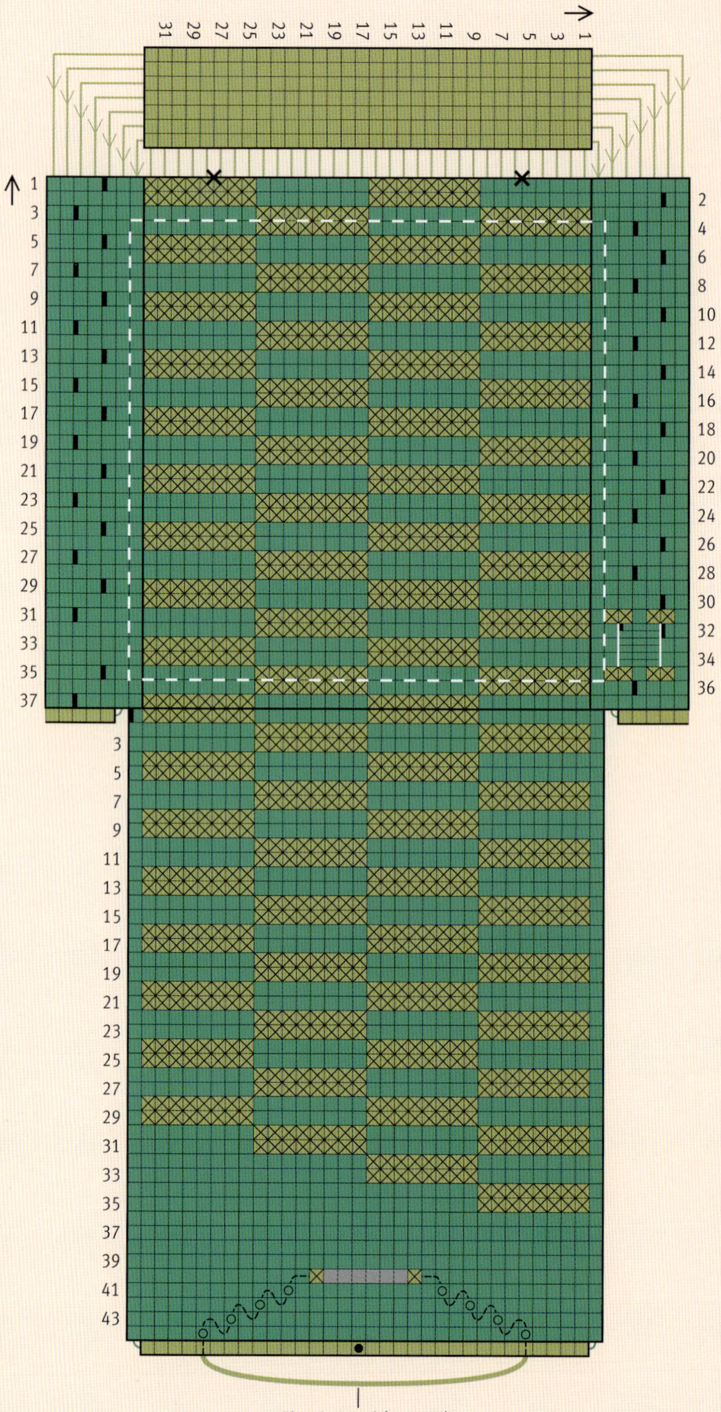

Thread Layout and Knotting Diagram for "Contemporary Design" (Page 60)

The knotting diagram shows the base, back side with the diagonally knotted case flap, the side sections, and the front side

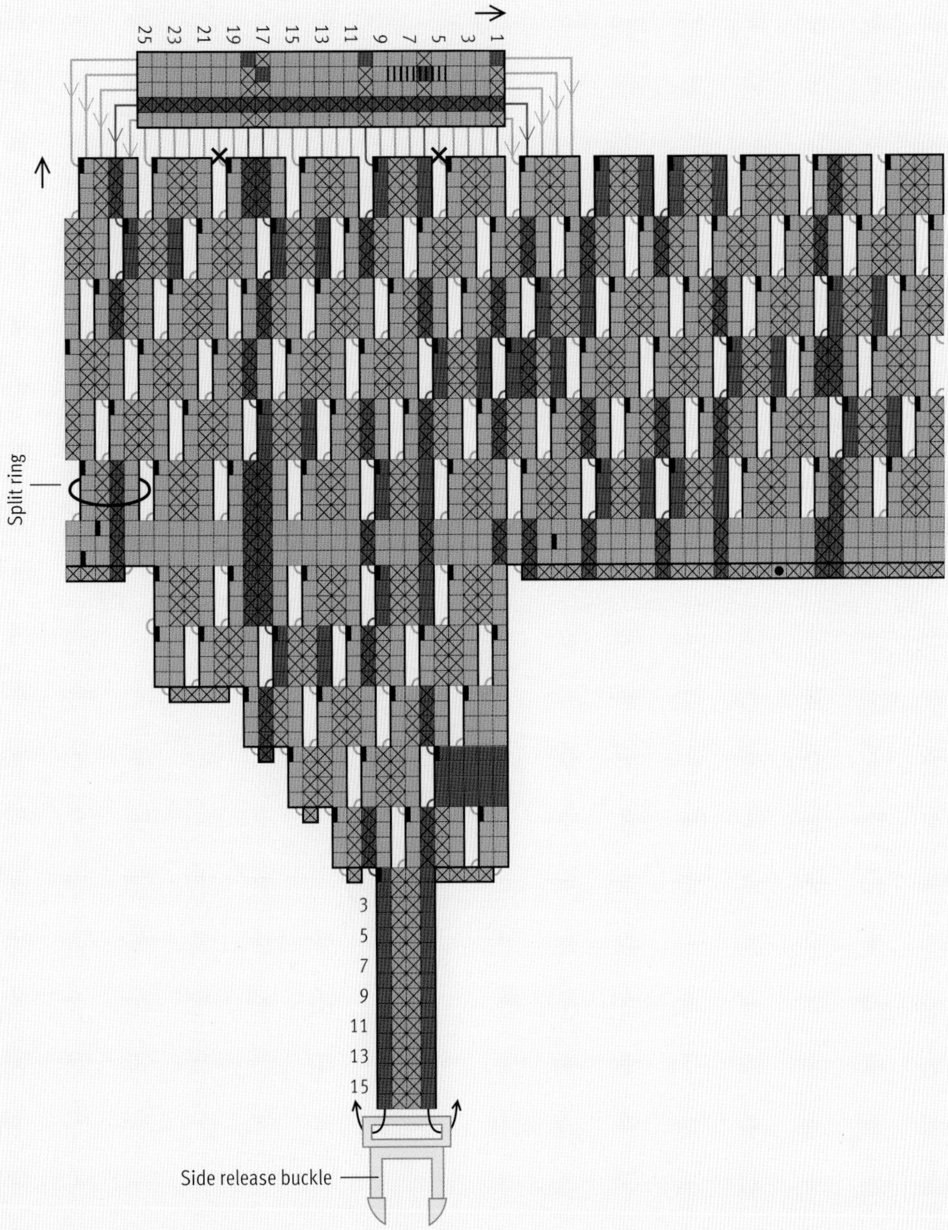

Thread Layout

For the Base and Case

- 24 core cords in gray (dark gray), about 8 feet (2.5 m) each
- 6 core cords in purple (white), about 8 feet (2.5 m) each

For the Top Case Border

- 2 knotting cords in gray (dark gray), about 5 feet (1.50 m) each

Key

- ↑ Direction
- ◧ Beginning of round, or rather row
- ✕ Auxiliary thread
- ☒ Horizontal half hitch knot
- ☐ Vertical half hitch knot
- ⊡ Finishing knot
- III Sew on the other piece of the side release buckle here

Contemporary Design

Materials

- $1\frac{3}{4}$ oz. (50 g) cotton each in gray (dark gray), purple (white)
- Side release buckle in white, $\frac{3}{8}$ inch (10 mm) wide
- Split ring, $\frac{1}{8}$ inch (4 mm) dia.

Thread Layout and Knotting Diagram
Page 59

Size
2 x $2\frac{3}{8}$ x $\frac{1}{4}$ inches
(5.2 cm x 6 cm x 0.7 cm)
(W x H x D)

Level of Difficulty
◆◆

1. According to the basic instructions (pages 6 - 13), first make the base of the case from 30 core cords (5 vertical threads, 25 horizontal threads). The 4th vertical and 1st, 6th, 10th, 17th, and 18th horizontal thread is purple (white).

2. Separate the core cords in 12 strands with 5 threads. The left thread from each 5 threads becomes the knotting cord. Make 2 forward rows and 1 backward row over the four right threads of the strand as per the knotting diagram. Work the following rows offset so that the hole pattern is formed (see knotting diagram).

3. On the left side, pull the split ring on a knotted flap made of the 5-strands. Now work 3 more rounds clockwise alternating with two knotting cords. Then stitch up all beginning and ending threads on the inside.

4. For the clasp flap on the back side of the case, separate the center 25 threads (basic instructions, page 12) and divide again in 5-strands. With the appropriate right threads knot over the remaining 4 threads of a strand according to the pattern.

5. So that the case flap is diagonal, from the 3rd round, leave the threads on the left side. With these threads, make a row of horizontal half hitch knots over the respective left thread. Then stitch up these threads on the back side.

6. After the 5th round, separate 5 threads for the flap and knot 8 forward and 8 backward rows with the left thread. Afterwards, with the threads of this narrow flap, stitch on the one piece of the side release buckle. Make 2 final rows on each left and right of the flap.

7. With the remaining core cords of the side sections and the front side, knot a final row towards the center of the front side. Finally, stitch up all threads on the inside. Sew on the other piece of the side release buckle on the front side (see knotting diagram).

Copyright © 2012 by Schiffer Publishing
Translated by: Christine Elliston
Originally published as *Knüpf-Design*
by Christophorus Verlag GmbH & Co. KG, Freiburg
Editing: Gisa Windhüfel, Freiburg
Photographs: Uwe Schotte, Nürnberg
Styling: Ingrid Schiller, Erlangen
Technical Illustrations: GrafikwerkFreiburg
Type set in Tartine Script Black/MetaCondNormalLF

Library of Congress Control Number: 2012931692

ISBN: 978-0-7643-3999-8
Printed in China

Schiffer Books are available at special discounts for bulk purchases for sales promotions or premiums. Special editions, including personalized covers, corporate imprints, and excerpts can be created in large quantities for special needs. For more information contact the publisher:

Schiffer Publishing Ltd.
4880 Lower Valley Road
Atglen, PA 19310
Phone: (610) 593-1777
Fax: (610) 593-2002
E-mail: Info@schifferbooks.com

For the largest selection of fine reference books on this and related subjects, please visit our website at
www.schifferbooks.com
We are always looking for people to write books on new and related subjects. If you have an idea for a book, please contact us at
proposals@schifferbooks.com

This book may be purchased from the publisher.
You may write for a free catalog.

In Europe, Schiffer books are distributed by

Bushwood Books
6 Marksbury Ave.
Kew Gardens
Surrey TW9 4JF England
Phone: 44 (0) 20 8392 8585
Fax: 44 (0) 20 8392 9876
E-mail: info@bushwoodbooks.co.uk
Website: www.bushwoodbooks.co.uk

More Schiffer Titles

www.schifferbooks.com

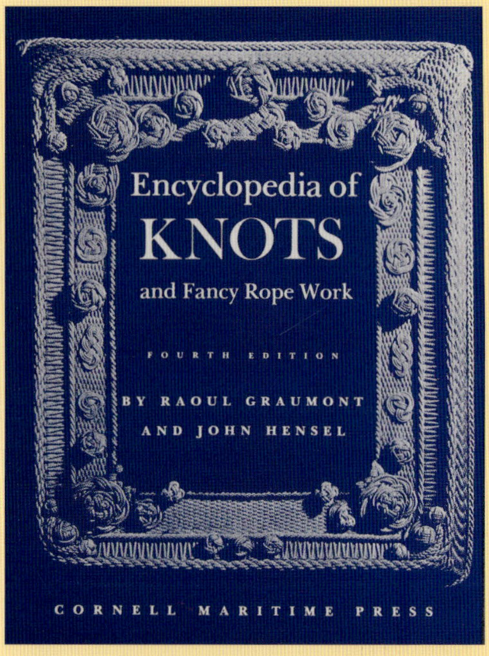

Macrame Today: Contemporary Knotting Projects. Darlyn Susan Yee. Knotting as an art form can be very diverse and result in a complex blend of texture and intricate patterns, using such materials as yarn, fiber, and string. With 110 color images and step-by-step instructions, this comprehensive guide provides artists and crafters with a platform for creating beautifully designed wearable and functional art pieces. Basic knotting is reviewed and ten projects of varying skill levels include bracelets, necklaces, scarf, cell phone pouch, and a yoga mat harness. Each chapter includes a list of supplies, materials, knotting techniques, and guidelines for successfully completing your very own creations.
Size: 8 1/2" x 11" • 110 color images • 64 pp.
ISBN: 978-0-7643-3799-4 • soft cover • $19.99

Encyclopedia of Knots and Fancy Rope Work. 4th Edition Raoul Graumont & John Hensel. This is unquestionably the greatest book on knots and rope work ever published, yet it is a valuable reference for anyone from eight to eighty. First published in 1939, it quickly became—and has remained for more than a half century—the classic in its field. Truly comprehensive in scope, this encyclopedia begins with a history of knots and rope making and proceeds into the how-to of tying and of making useful and decorative articles with rope. More than 3,600 knots are described and illustrated in 348 full-page plates.
Size: 7 1/4" x 9 5/8" • 4,501 illustrations, 7 b/w photos • Glossary/Index • 704 pp.
ISBN: 978-0-87033-021-6 • hard cover • $39.95

Schiffer books may be ordered from your local bookstore, or they may be ordered directly from the publisher by writing to:
Schiffer Publishing, Ltd.
4880 Lower Valley Rd.
Atglen, PA 19310
(610) 593-1777; Fax (610) 593-2002
E-mail: Info@schifferbooks.com

Please visit our website catalog at *www.schifferbooks.com* or write for a free catalog.

Printed in China